Political Games

Political Games

Strategy, Persuasion, and Learning

Special Issue Editors

Gabriele Gratton
Galina Zudenkova

MDPI • Basel • Beijing • Wuhan • Barcelona • Belgrade • Manchester • Tokyo • Cluj • Tianjin

Special Issue Editors

Gabriele Gratton
School of Economics,
UNSW Business School,
UNSW Sydney
Australia

Galina Zudenkova
Faculty of Business and
Economics, TU Dortmund
University
Germany

Editorial Office
MDPI
St. Alban-Anlage 66
4052 Basel, Switzerland

This is a reprint of articles from the Special Issue published online in the open access journal *Games* (ISSN 2073-4336) (available at: https://www.mdpi.com/journal/games/special_issues/Political_Games).

For citation purposes, cite each article independently as indicated on the article page online and as indicated below:

LastName, A.A.; LastName, B.B.; LastName, C.C. Article Title. *Journal Name* **Year**, *Article Number*, Page Range.

ISBN 978-3-03928-446-7 (Pbk)
ISBN 978-3-03928-447-4 (PDF)

Cover image courtesy of Marco Oriolesi on Unsplash.com.

© 2020 by the authors. Articles in this book are Open Access and distributed under the Creative Commons Attribution (CC BY) license, which allows users to download, copy and build upon published articles, as long as the author and publisher are properly credited, which ensures maximum dissemination and a wider impact of our publications.
The book as a whole is distributed by MDPI under the terms and conditions of the Creative Commons license CC BY-NC-ND.

Contents

About the Special Issue Editors vii

Gabriele Gratton and Galina Zudenkova
Introduction to the Special Issue Political Games: Strategy, Persuasion, and Learning
Reprinted from: *Games* **2020**, *11*, 10, doi:10.3390/g11010010 1

Giovanna M. Invernizzi
Public Information: Relevance or Salience?
Reprinted from: *Games* **2020**, *11*, 4, doi:10.3390/g11010004 3

Jacopo Bizzotto and Benjamin Solow
Electoral Competition with Strategic Disclosure
Reprinted from: *Games* **2019**, *10*, 29, doi:10.3390/g10030029 31

Addison Pan
A Note on Pivotality
Reprinted from: *Games* **2019**, *10*, 24, doi:10.3390/g10020024 49

Marco Serena
A Game-Free Microfoundation of Mutual Optimism
Reprinted from: *Games* **2019**, *10*, 37, doi:10.3390/g10040037 57

About the Special Issue Editors

Gabriele Gratton is Scientia Fellow Associate Professor of Economics at UNSW Sydney. He received his PhD from Boston University. His research focuses on information asymmetries and communication in politics and organizations. Through his research, Gabriele Gratton aims to understand how the institutions and technologies controlling the transmission of information affect election campaigns and policymaking. More broadly, he is interested in the role played by noisy information in politics, from armed conflicts to voting.

Galina Zudenkova is Professor of Public Finance at the TU Dortmund University, Germany. She received her PhD from University Carlos III of Madrid. Her research interests lie in the areas of Public Economics, Political Economy, and Institutional Economics. Within these fields, she focuses on the game theoretical analysis of the interactions between agents in economic and political environments and test empirically the derived hypotheses. In her previous and current research, she studies the questions of policy choice and policy implementation with the focus on principal-agent relationships, redistribution, public good provision, politician selection and institutional regime change.

Editorial

Introduction to the Special Issue Political Games: Strategy, Persuasion, and Learning

Gabriele Gratton [1,*] and Galina Zudenkova [2]

1. UNSW Business School, UNSW Sydney, Sydney, NSW 20152, Australia
2. TU Dortmund University, D-44227 Dortmund, Germany; galina.zudenkova@tu-dortmund.de
* Correspondence: g.gratton@unsw.edu.au

Received: 26 January 2020; Accepted: 1 February 2020; Published: 7 February 2020

All political actors, from world leaders to common citizens, make choices based on information that is noisy, perhaps biased, and sometimes fake. In recent decades, widespread Internet use, the multiplication of specialized TV channels, and the rise of social media have fundamentally changed the way in which political actors collect and disseminate information. Political pundits and academics thus question whether common wisdom about media and political campaigns remains valid in this new environment of information and communication technologies (see, for example, [1–4]).

This Special Issue is a collection of articles that contribute to this debate, combining game-theoretical and experimental work. One piece of common wisdom is that electoral campaigns are swayed by public events such as endorsements by newspapers or celebrities. However, there is broad disagreement about why these public acts are particularly salient to voters. One theory is that voters believe that endorsements convey precise signals about key political issues debated during the campaign or about the relative quality of candidates. The opposing view is that these events serve as coordination devices for voters, independently of whether they are informative or not. Supporters of the latter view often point out that some salient events appear to be obviously uninformative.

In this Special Issue, Invernizzi [5] developed a clever series of experiments to test these two theories. Interestingly, she reports rather mixed evidence. In accordance with the first theory, the more informative the public signal is, the more the voters follow it. However, voters do not do so in the systematic way the theory would predict. In addition, voters' response is quite heterogeneous and therefore they fail to fully use the signal as a coordination device. Instead, the experiment reveals that what determines the voters' behavior in a homogeneous and significant way is the signal's recency. In all experiments in [5], almost every single subject follows the most recent signal with staggering regularity, regardless of the signal's precision. This finding raises new questions on the timing of information revelation in electoral campaigns, casting further concerns about manipulation of voting behavior (see, for example, [6,7]).

Bizzotto and Solow [8] dug deeper into the question of information manipulation during electoral campaigns. They noticed that campaigns are naturally multidimensional and that different voters care about different dimensions. In this context, the rise of social media and the availability of the individual data that come with it allow candidates to "microtarget" their campaign messages, i.e., to send different messages to different groups of voters. Bizzotto and Solow [8] found that such microtargeting is generically socially inefficient as it gives the candidates an incentive to commit to socially inefficient projects that benefit specific groups of voters. This result adds to the public debate on the role of social media in recent elections and may inform policymakers who wish to regulate individual data use for political campaigns (see, for example, [9]).

While political actors can manipulate or target information during electoral campaigns, electoral outcomes are solely determined by the voters' choices. Since the work of Austen-Smith and Banks [10], game-theoretical models have analyzed voting decisions in common value elections. The standard assumption in this literature is that voters are Bayesian expected utility maximizers. However, behavioral economics suggests that individuals behave very differently when they are uncertain about the information structure, i.e., when the environment is *ambiguous*. Recently, Ellis [11] extended the analysis of strategic voting in common value elections to ambiguous environments with ambiguity-averse voters. In this Special Issue, Pan [12] concisely provided a general description of such ambiguous voting games and derived general equilibrium conditions for them.

Deviations from rationality are also often considered as possible causes for Pareto inefficient conflicts. In particular, one oft-cited explanation for conflict is that players are *mutually optimistic*, i.e., each side expects to prevail in the ensuing conflict. However, why would world leaders have such inconsistent beliefs? In this Special Issue, Serena [13] developed the idea that such beliefs are formed as a result of a particular form of information naivety when players systematically fail to draw correct inference about each other's private information from each other's action. To put it bluntly, when the two sides do not "read" into each other's actions, then mutual optimism is a natural result, thus leading to Pareto inefficient conflicts.

In conclusion, the four articles in this Special Issue contribute to our understanding of the role of information structure and belief formation in political games. The articles promote novel ideas and address understudied questions, which range from salience determination to microtargeting, ambiguous voting, and information naivety. The findings complement the existing literature and suggest rationales for inefficiencies that arise in political environments with incomplete and noisy information.

Conflicts of Interest: The authors declare no conflict of interest.

References

1. Allcott, H.; Gentzkow, M. Social Media and Fake News in the 2016 Election. *J. Econ. Perspect.* **2017**, *31*, 211–236. [CrossRef]
2. Gentzkow, M.; Shapiro, J.M. Ideological Segregation Online and Offline. *Q. J. Econ.* **2011**, *126*, 1799–1839. [CrossRef]
3. Townsend, T. The Bizarre Truth Behind the Biggest Pro-Trump Facebook Hoaxes. *Inc.*, 21 November 2016.
4. Wingfield, N.; Isaac, M.; Benner, K. Google and Facebook Take Aim at Fake News Sites. *New York Times*, 14 November 2016.
5. Invernizzi, G.M. Public Information: Relevance or Salience? *Games* **2020**, *11*, 4. [CrossRef]
6. Guttman, I.; Kremer, I.; Skrzypacz, A. Not Only What but Also When: A Theory of Dynamic Voluntary Disclosure. *Am. Econ. Rev.* **2014**, *104*, 2400–2420. [CrossRef]
7. Gratton, G.; Holden, R.; Kolotilin, A. When to Drop a Bombshell. *Rev. Econ. Stud.* **2018**, *85*, 2139–2172. [CrossRef]
8. Bizzotto, J.; Solow, B. Electoral Competition with Strategic Disclosure. *Games* **2019**, *10*, 29. [CrossRef]
9. Aral, S.; Eckles, D. Protecting Elections from Social Media Manipulation. *Science* **2019**, *365*, 858–861. [CrossRef] [PubMed]
10. Austen-Smith, D.; Banks, J.S. Information Aggregation, Rationality, and the Condorcet Jury Theorem. *Am. Political Sci. Rev.* **1996**, *90*, 34–45. [CrossRef]
11. Ellis, A. Condorcet Meets Ellsberg. *Theor. Econ.* **2016**, *11*, 865–895. [CrossRef]
12. Pan, A. A Note on Pivotality. *Games* **2019**, *10*, 24. [CrossRef]
13. Serena, M. A Game-Free Microfoundation of Mutual Optimism. *Games* **2019**, *10*, 37. [CrossRef]

© 2020 by the authors. Licensee MDPI, Basel, Switzerland. This article is an open access article distributed under the terms and conditions of the Creative Commons Attribution (CC BY) license (http://creativecommons.org/licenses/by/4.0/).

Article
Public Information: Relevance or Salience?

Giovanna M. Invernizzi [†]

Political Science Department, Columbia University, 420 W 118th St., New York, NY 10027, USA; giovanna.invernizzi@columbia.edu

† I would like to offer my special thanks to Alessandra Casella, Judd Kessler, Mark Dean, Silvio Ravaioli, Pietro Ortoleva and participants of the Experimental Economics Seminar at Columbia for valuable and constructive suggestions. I thank participants to seminars and conferences in Harvard HEWG, Princeton PE research group, SWEET New York, BMP Rice and EITM Summer Institute for their helpful comments.

Received: 27 July 2019; Accepted: 19 November 2019; Published: 6 January 2020

Abstract: How does salient public information affect voters' behavior? In a majoritarian voting game with common preferences, rational voters could use public information as an information device (depending on accuracy) or as a coordination device (regardless of accuracy). A simple lab experiment contradicts both hypotheses – subjects tend to follow public information when it is salient, regardless of the information's accuracy, but fail to use it as a source of coordination. In particular, it matters whether the information is recent – subjects are more likely to follow public information when it is provided closer to the voting decision. These findings are important because the salience of public information is easily manipulable by political actors.

Keywords: information aggregation; committee decision making; voting experiment; recency bias

1. Introduction

When voters have to decide over issues of common interest, they often find themselves influenced by visible events of debatable direct relevance. Before winning the Democratic nomination in 2008, Obama was endorsed by Oprah Winfrey in Iowa, and the endorsement was one of the most widely covered developments of the campaign—Reference [1] estimated that Oprah's endorsement was responsible for approximately 1 million additional votes for Obama. During the 2016 EU referendum in England, Roger Daltrey (lead singer of the iconic rock band The Who) explained in an interview by The Mirror why he thought Brexit was the right thing to do.[1] These examples share the attribute that the information provided is public and *salient*, particularly noticeable. In the case of the endorsement to Obama, voters might have seen it as an informative public signal, thinking that Oprah had precise information about the candidate, or as a coordination device, believing that everyone else observed it. Alternatively, they could have paid attention to the endorsement because it was extremely noticeable, as Oprah is a famous celebrity and the endorsement happened right before the election.

This paper uses a laboratory experiment to study salient public information and voters' decision: the main finding of the experiment is that recency bias largely affects collective decision making.

There are three main explanations for why salient public information could be influential. First, if the information provided is more accurate than voters' private information, then voters may trust the public source more. Second, public information can serve as a coordination mechanism for voters, who may then rationally choose to disregard their private information and follow the public source

---

[1] The article can be found here: https://www.mirror.co.uk/news/uk-news/who-legend-roger-daltrey-hes-8252353. There were several other instances of this kind. Google searches for celebrities and Brexit peaked in the week before the referendum, and many web pages displayed long lists of Brexit's supporters.

even when the latter is not accurate. Finally, salient public information can be influential because of biases or heuristics affecting voters' decision. This paper analyzes each of these explanations.

Salience of information affects how people focus their limited cognitive resources. Salience bias (or perceptual salience) refers to the fact that individuals focus more on information that is striking and perceptible and ignore information that is less so.[2] One attribute of salience that is particularly effective in politics is recency. According to the recency bias (or availability heuristic), people tend to heavily weight their judgments towards information received more recently, making new opinions biased toward latest news.[3] Public information delivered close to the vote (as Oprah's endorsement) can be overweighted by voters, who have it readily available in their short-term memory. In real-world situations it is hard to tell why voters respond to salient public information. In particular, it is difficult to separate the importance of the way information is framed from its content, as typically the two come together.[4] This experiment is designed precisely to overcome this challenge.

I begin with the canonical majority rule committee setting, where voting aggregates members' independent signals about the state of the world [9,10]. When in addition a public signal is observed by everyone, voters could use the public information as an information device (depending on accuracy) or as a coordination device (regardless of accuracy). In a recent paper, Reference [11]—henceforth KV—noticed that if the public signal is more precise than each private signal, then majority rule no longer leads to an equilibrium in which every voter always votes according to the private signal. In this setting, there exist a *responsive* equilibrium where voters change their vote as a function of their own private signals with positive probability, for values of the public signal's accuracy below a certain threshold. Moreover, for any relative accuracy of the two signals, (non-responsive) *conformist* equilibria exist where voters coordinate on the basis of the public information without considering their private signals.

To these two possible roles of the public signal—information and coordination—a laboratory experiment superimposes a third element: salience. Subjects face structurally equivalent games which differ in the salience of the information provided. One salience treatment is designed to explicitly capture subjects' attention, by emphasizing the information with graphics and music. Another treatment changes the relative timing of private and public signals. If subjects behaved according to the equilibrium predictions, their behavior would not change substantially across different salience treatments. If, on the other hand, subjects were to process information according to salience bias, we would expect more votes for the public signal when this is salient.

The experimental results show that subjects' behavior is responsive to signals' precision: when the public signal is more accurate than the private, subjects follow it more than when it is less accurate than the private one. Yet, the behavior observed is far from the responsive equilibrium predictions. Subjects' behavior also contradicts the coordination mechanism: although the conformist equilibrium is not responsive to signals' relative precision, subjects' behavior is. Results, instead, point towards the role of salience of information. In particular, the order of message delivery matters: subjects tend to follow the public signal more when it is the most recent signal observed before voting. Recency has a substantive and statistically significant impact on subjects' behavior: in all the experimental sessions subjects follow the most recent signal (the last signal observed before voting) 75% of the time, regardless of the signal's precision. Moreover, recency has a striking homogeneous effect: the proportion of votes with the public signal under the recency treatment is greater than the proportion of votes with the public signal when this is displayed before the private one, for almost every subject in the experiment and

---

[2] For a discussion of how salience can affect individual decision making, see References [2,3].
[3] For experimental evidence of recency bias on individual decision making, see References [4,5]. Reference [6] model recency effects as exogenous weighting of evidence. For a formal model that generates recency effects as a result of Bayesian updating, see Reference [7].
[4] This challenge is posed by Reference [8], who suggests that to isolate framing mechanisms, one would need to study the effect of completely uninformative events.

regardless of signals' relative accuracy. Interestingly, this result is robust to additional sessions where subjects do not vote in committees over issues of common interest, making individual choices instead. Finding the same behavior in the individual sessions suggests that coordination on public information does not explain subjects' behavior.

This paper relates to the literature studying salience bias in voters' decisions. In particular, recency effects have been studied in the context of electoral campaigns. Reference [12] analyze a sender-receiver game connecting the timing of information release with voter beliefs prior to elections. They formally derive an equilibrium in which fabricated scandals are only released close to the election date, and confirm their equilibrium prediction using data on the release of US presidential scandals. Timing of message delivery in electoral campaigns has also been the subject of field experiments [13,14]. Reference [13] studies the effect of phone calls by volunteers on voter turnout. The experiment shows how calls made during the final days prior to the election are most effective in mobilizing voters, and that the specific content of the conversation is less important than the timing of the call. This paper's contribution is to provide a controlled experimental test of the role of salient public information on voting. While in field experiments it is hard to isolate the importance of salience from the informational content a message provides, this experimental design overcomes this challenge.

The paper also relates to the literature on committee decision making in voting experiments. Specifically, KV focus on the information and coordination mechanisms with private and public signals and show with a laboratory experiment that voters might be drawn to inefficient conformist equilibria where private information is ignored and voters conform to the public signal. While the main focus of this experiment is the role of salience of the public signals, some of the findings replicate the general result and other specific findings in KV: one treatment considers a public signal that is less precise than voters' private signals, and another one presents the same public information as a common asymmetric prior instead of a public signal.

The fundamental contribution of this paper is its focus on the role of salience. The treatments are designed to raise the salience of the public message by changing when it is displayed (recency) and by using entertaining music and animations—which makes this experimental design unique. Interestingly, results show that salience treatment effects decayed over time. One interpretation of this result is that salience represents novelty, and as such it should decline with repeated treatments. Furthermore, it is noteworthy that the same salience effects hold when subjects face an individual-decision making problem, without involving groups or pivotality calculations.

Finally, the experiment shows that recency bias is a persistent presence in voters' decision-making. When making important decisions such as voting, people may focus on features that are easy to process and vivid because available in short-term memory, rather than more informative but less salient ones. This bias in information processing can lead to suboptimal decisions. Knowing this, politicians and media can shift voters' attention to events that take place at crucial times. As Oprah's endorsement illustrated, endorsements are strategically timed to be maximally effective. The fact that such signals may be more effective the closer they are to voters' decision is important, and a novel fining for empirical research on endorsements.

The remainder of the paper is organized as follows. The next section describes the theoretical model and equilibrium predictions. The following sections present experimental design and results. The last section concludes. Proofs, additional data and a copy of the experimental instructions are reported in Appendix A.

2. The Model

This section formally derives the theoretical predictions that are tested in the laboratory experiment. The same results have been derived in KV and Reference [15], and have been recently extended in Reference [16].

Consider a committee that consists of n members, where n is odd. Agents make a collective decision $d \in \mathcal{D} = \{A, B\}$ over two alternatives. The state of the world is $\omega \in \Omega = \{A, B\}$. Both events are ex ante equally likely: $Pr(A) = Pr(B) = \pi = 0.5$, where π is the common prior.

Each agent casts a vote for one of the two alternatives $\{A, B\}$:[5] we define the individual vote $d_i = a$ if the agent votes in favor of alternative A, and $d_i = b$ otherwise. The committee decides by majority voting. Committee members have identical preferences, and payoffs are normalized without loss of generality to 0 or 1. Specifically, I denote by $u_i(d, \omega)$ the utility to voter i of decision d in state ω and assume $u_i(A, A) = u_i(B, B) = 1$ and $u_i(A, B) = u_i(B, A) = 0$ for each member of the committee. This means each agent wants the collective decision to match the state of the world.

Agents receive two pieces of information before voting: a private and a public signal. The private signal is denoted by $s_i \in S_i = \{\alpha, \beta\}$. The probability of the signal matching the state is symmetric across the two states and given by $Pr[s_i = \alpha|A] = Pr[s_i = \beta|B] = q \in (\frac{1}{2}, 1)$. The public signal is denoted by $s_p \in S_p = \{\alpha, \beta\}$, with $Pr[s_p = \alpha|A] = Pr[s_p = \beta|B] = Q \in (\frac{1}{2}, 1)$. Private signals are conditionally independent across voters, and the public signal is conditionally independent from the private signals.

Notice that, without public signals, there exists an equilibrium where each voter follows her private signal and—as the number of committee members grows—the probability that the majority takes the correct decision tends to one [9,10].

The timing of the game is as follows:

1. Nature determines the state of the world ω.
2. Each voter observes a private signal and the public signal (observed by everyone).
3. Agents cast their votes and the collective decision d is determined according to the majority of votes.
4. The true state is revealed and agents receive their payoffs.

A (mixed) voting strategy $v_i : S_i \times S_p \to [0, 1]$ defines the probability that each agent votes for the public signal s_p, given the realization of both private and public signals. For instance, $v_i(\alpha, \beta)$ indicates the probability that i votes for B given that $s_i = \alpha$ and $s_p = \beta$.

The next section considers how voting behavior changes depending on the signals agents receive. Agent i's vote depends on the content of the two signals observed, and whether they agree ($s_i = s_p$) or disagree ($s_i \neq s_p$). Notice that the case $v_i(s_i = \alpha, s_p = \alpha)$ is equivalent to $v_i(s_i = \beta, s_p = \beta)$, because the model is symmetric with respect to the two states A and B. Similarly, $v_i(s_i = \alpha, s_p = \beta)$ is equivalent to $v_i(s_i = \beta, s_p = \alpha)$.

Equilibrium Analysis

Define by $\gamma \in [0, 1]$ the probability that a voter votes according to the public signal when the two signals agree, and $\mu \in [0, 1]$ the probability that she votes according to the public signal when private and public signals disagree.

Definition 1. *A voting strategy is symmetric if $v_i(\alpha, \alpha) = v_i(\beta, \beta) \equiv \gamma$ and $v_i(\alpha, \beta) = v_i(\beta, \alpha) \equiv \mu$ for every i.*

Definition 2. *A voting strategy is responsive if $v_i(\alpha, s_p) \neq v_i(\beta, s_p)$ for every s_p.*

Definition 3. *A profile of strategies $\mathbf{S}$ is more informative than $\mathbf{S}'$ if*

$$Pr(d = \omega|\mathbf{S}) > Pr(d = \omega|\mathbf{S}').$$

---

[5] Assume that voters cannot abstain, and that there is no cost of casting votes.

That is, an equilibrium is more informative than another if it uses more information and gets to the right decision more often. I will first restrict the analysis to the most informative symmetric equilibrium, which can be (but not necessarily is) responsive to private information. In a symmetric responsive equilibrium, voters' strategies are sensitive to private signals (and all individuals use the same strategy).

The first result shows that, when the public signal's precision is low enough, in the most informative equilibrium voters always follow the private signal.

Lemma 1. *When $Q \leq q$, the most informative symmetric equilibrium is the unique responsive equilibrium where agents always vote with their private signal.*

Proof. All proofs are in the Appendix A, unless otherwise noted. □

To get the intuition for Lemma 1, consider the decision of a voter. Under the event of pivotality, half of the other voters vote for A and half for B. The voter observes the public and private signals, which differ. Given that the other votes are collectively uninformative, the voter follows the most precise signal between the private and the public. Hence, if the private signal is more precise than the public one, following the public signal is strictly dominated.

In what follows, consider the case in which the public signal is more precise than the private, that is, $Q > q$. The next result shows that there exist a mixed strategy equilibrium in which voters follow the public signal with positive probability (smaller than one), provided that the precision of the public signal is lower than a threshold, Q^H, defined below.

Proposition 1 (Symmetric Responsive Equilibrium). *When $Q \in (q, Q^H]$ the most informative symmetric equilibrium is the unique responsive equilibrium where $\gamma = 1$ when private and public signals agree; when private and public signals disagree, agents vote according to the public signal with probability*

$$\mu = \frac{\gamma - q(1+\gamma)}{1 - q - q\gamma},$$

where $\gamma(q, Q, N) = \left(\frac{q/1-q}{Q/1-Q}\right)^{\frac{2}{N-1}} \frac{q}{(1-q)}$. The threshold Q_H is given by

$$Q^H = \frac{1}{1 + \left(\left(-1 + \frac{1}{q}\right)^{\frac{1+n}{1-n}}\right)^{\frac{1-n}{2}}}.$$

Notice that the voting profile described by Proposition 1 prescribes to vote according to the public signal with positive probability only if $Q > q$. When $Q \leq q$, Lemma 1 shows that the voter's dominant strategy is to follow the private signal. The last case to consider is when the public signal precision is above Q^H.

Corollary 1. *When $Q > Q^H$ there exists no symmetric responsive equilibrium, and in the most informative symmetric equilibrium agents always vote with the public signal.*

We can summarize the predictions for the most informative symmetric equilibrium as follows:

1. if $s_i = s_p$, players' best response is to follow both signals
2. if $s_i \neq s_p$, then:

    (a) if $Q \leq q$, always follow the private signal ($\mu = 0$),
    (b) if $Q \in (q, Q^H]$, follow s_p with probability $\mu \in (0, 1)$,
    (c) if $Q > Q^H$ always follow the public signal ($\mu = 1$).

Besides the most informative symmetric equilibrium, which can be responsive or not, there exist other symmetric equilibria where voters conform to the public signal. Notice that these equilibria are not responsive, that is, agents do not change their vote as a function of their own signal with positive probability.

Proposition 2 (Conformist Equilibrium). *There exists a symmetric Bayesian Nash equilibrium in which every agent votes according to (against) the public signal.*

Proof. Consider the choice of an individual i. If every other agent votes according to (against) the public signal, agent i is not pivotal and therefore she is indifferent about which alternative to vote for. Thus every agent voting according to (against) the public signal is an equilibrium. □

Conformist equilibria can be very inefficient, especially when the public signal is below the threshold Q^H determined above. That is, introducing a public signal may be deleterious because the public signal might be seen as a focal point which makes coordination easier for committee members, thus hindering information aggregation.

In addition to the two symmetric equilibria in Proposition 2, there exist several asymmetric ones where voters conform to the public signal.[6] However, these equilibria do not seem to be very plausible. In particular, as described in the experimental setting below, groups are randomly matched in each period: because it is difficult to coordinate on asymmetric equilibria with random matching, these asymmetric equilibria are very unlikely to emerge.

3. Experimental Design

The experiment is designed to answer two questions. The first asks to what extent subjects' behavior responds to signals' precision. In particular, the experiment tests whether subjects vote according to the public signal when they know that it is less precise than their private ones. The first treatment of interest changes the relative precision of the private and public signals. Since there is no evidence of learning in the data (see Appendix A), I report the results below aggregating over all rounds of the same treatment. The second question asks how salience of public information affects voting behavior. To understand the impact of salience, I create five structurally equivalent games (corresponding to different treatments), in which public information is provided in different ways.

The experiment was organized in ten separate sessions, all held at the Columbia Experimental Laboratory (CELSS). Subjects were registered students, recruited through the laboratory web site. No subject participated in more than one session. Overall, 157 subjects participated in the experiment. The experiment was conducted using the software Z-Tree [17], and a copy of the instructions is presented in Appendix A. Each session lasted about one hour, and earnings ranged from $18 to $28, with an average of $24 (including a $5 show-up fee).

Each session was comprised of 70 rounds. In every round, participants were randomly matched with each other to form a committee of 5 members.[7] Subjects were told that their group's task was to find a prize (worth 70 experimental dollars) which was hidden in one of two boxes, one red, one blue. The computer placed the prize in the red box with probability 50%, and each subject received two pieces of information: a private message and a public message. To make clear that the public message was common knowledge, all public messages were displayed on the two central screens of

---

[6] For instance, consider a committee of five members where each member observes a private signal and everyone observes the same public signal. One equilibrium is that one member of the committee votes with her private signal, when this disagrees with the public, and the other four members vote with (against) the public signal. In another equilibrium, two committee members vote with their private signals, which disagree with the public, and the other three members of the committee vote with (against) the public signal.

[7] This is true for the first four sessions. As displayed in Table 1 and explained later, in sessions 5–10 there were no committees and subjects performed an individual task.

the laboratory. The private messages were displayed on each subjects' monitor. After receiving the information, subjects voted for either the red box or the blue box.[8] The alternative that received the majority of votes was selected. After every round, subjects received feedback about the number of votes cast by their group for the red and blue box, whether the group decision was correct or not, and their earnings for the round. Individual payoffs were based on whether the group decision was correct or incorrect: 70 experimental dollars for each correct decision, 10 experimental dollars for a wrong decision. Subjects were paid the sum of their round earnings.

Table 1 shows which sessions had high public signal accuracy ($Q = 0.7$), and low ($Q = 0.55$). The accuracy of the private signal was set to $q = 0.6$ throughout all sessions. The committee size was set to $n = 5$ for the entire experiment. For these parameters, the equilibrium predictions for the symmetric responsive equilibrium are to follow the public signal 37% of the time when this is more precise than the private ($Q > q$), and never follow it when $Q \leq q$. According to the equilibrium in which subjects coordinate on (against) the public signal, everybody (nobody) follows the public signal when the two signals disagree, even when the public signal is less accurate than the private.

Table 1. Summary of experimental sessions. The accuracy of the private signal was set to $q = 0.6$ throughout the whole experiment. A total of 75 subjects were assigned to a "group" condition, and divided in committees of size five. The other 82 subjects were assigned to an "individual" condition.

Session	Q	Committee, Size	# Rounds	# Subjects
s_1	0.7	Yes, 5	70	20
s_2	0.55	Yes, 5	70	20
s_3	0.7	Yes, 5	70	20
s_4	0.55	Yes, 5	70	15
s_5	0.7	No	70	13
s_6	0.55	No	70	17
s_7	0.7	No	70	10
s_8	0.55	No	70	16
s_9	0.7	No	70	13
s_{10}	0.55	No	70	13

In addition to testing how subject behavior changes with signal relative accuracy, this experiment studies how salience affects voting decision. Salience is defined along two dimensions. The first is recency, or timing relative to voting. I hypothesize that subjects follow more the message that is closer to the vote, because they have the information more readily available in their short-term memory [18–20]. The second dimension refers to how information is presented. Information that is visibly stunning is salient, because individuals focus more on items that are striking and perceptible [21]: as a consequence, subjects should overemphasize the information on which their minds focus.[9] The experimental treatments varying the two dimensions of recency and emphasis are described below.

Recency. This treatment varied whether the public signal was displayed before or after the private signal.

Asymmetric Prior. The least salient way to convey the public message is not to show it at all. This treatment corresponds to the last 10 rounds of each session. In these rounds, an asymmetric prior was provided instead of a symmetric ($\pi = 0.5$) prior, and no public signal was displayed. Subjects were told that the computer placed the prize in the blue box with probability $\pi = 0.7$

---

[8] The position of the vote buttons was randomly shuffled in each round.
[9] Reference [2] formalize this assumption in a model where decision makers overweight states that draw their attention by comparing payoff magnitude in different lotteries. This experimental treatment manipulates salience by changing the way information is presented, rather than payoffs.

(or $\pi = 0.55$, depending on the session), and in each round each subject received only a private signal. From a Bayesian standpoint, these ten rounds conveyed the same information as the previous ones: having a symmetric prior and a public signal with accuracy $Q = 0.7$ is identical to having an asymmetric prior $\pi = 0.7$ and no public signal. After receiving the private message, subjects were asked to vote for one of the two boxes, as in the first part of the experiment.

Jingle. This treatment varied the way the public signal was projected on the central screens. In the absence of this treatment, the public signal was displayed with the picture of a blue or red box (as for the private signals projected on subjects' monitors). With the *jingle* treatment, the public message was projected on the central screen with a video displaying a star jumping within an empty, white box, which then became either red or blue. The video was accompanied by a striking soundtrack, and to make the jingle treatment less repetitive, the music theme varied. I used famous music pieces such as Also sprach Zarathustra by Strauss, Eye of the tiger, The final Countdown, Thrift Shop and the Game of Thrones' soundtrack.[10] I hypothesize that salience of the public signal is increasing in both recency and emphasis.

Subjects in different sessions were presented with the same five treatments.[11] Each subject played thirty rounds with the public signal displayed before the private, and thirty with the private displayed before the public. Among each of these thirty rounds, eight displayed the public message with the jingle, so that it is possible to evaluate the interaction between jingle and recency treatments. I decided to keep the number of jingle rounds small to ensure novelty and subjects' interest. These conditions (recency, jingle) were randomly selected in every round, a feature designed to keep subjects engaged in the task. The only condition that was not randomly assigned is the asymmetric prior treatment, which consisted in the last ten rounds that every subject played. This design feature was chosen for feasibility, as it would not be possible to switch priors and signal structure in every round. Table 2 shows the number of rounds for each of the treatments.

Table 2. Factorial design for every session (for both $Q > q$ and $Q \leq q$). The row values are associated to the recency treatment (i.e., whether the private signal was displayed before or after the public). The column values are associated with the jingle treatment. The values within the matrix display the number of rounds for each interaction.

	Jingle	No Jingle
Asymmetric prior	-	10 rounds
Public first	8 rounds	22 rounds
Private first	8 rounds	22 rounds

4. Results

The first treatment of interest is designed to test whether subjects in committees follow more the public signal when it is more accurate than the private. I begin by aggregating the data across the salience treatments, given that salience is irrelevant according to the theory. Figure 1 displays the fraction of votes cast according to the public signal when the private and public signals disagree (estimated μ), as well as when the two signals agree. The second panel gives us a measure of the extent of pure noise in the experiment.

The first thing to notice is that the treatment effect goes in the expected direction: subjects vote more with the public signal when this is more precise than the private one (21% vs. 66%, statistically significant at any conventional level). However, the observed behavior is far from the symmetric responsive equilibrium predictions (red line in Figure 1), as well as from the conformist equilibria.

---

[10] All the videos are available upon request.
[11] Administering the salience treatments within subjects was a natural choice to get more data points under the time and budget constraints.

In particular, it is worth noting that 21% of the subjects vote according to the public signal even when this is less precise than the private one, when the two disagree (left column, left plot). When presented with the trivial choice of voting after receiving two identical signals, subjects tend to vote according to both. Nevertheless, even in this case subjects commit mistakes, quantified in the right plot by the distance between the bars and the blue lines (less than 10%).

Given this result, the mechanism according to which voters follow public signals because of their informativeness seems to lack explanatory power.[12] It might be that subjects are influenced by public information because of conformity, or because of bias in information processing. We know there exist two symmetric conformist equilibria with coordination on (or against) the public signal, and several asymmetric equilibria. However, all of these equilibria are not responsive to the relative precision of the two signals. Since we clearly see that the behavior of voters responds to signals' relative precision (treatment effect in Figure 1), all the non-responsive equilibria do not reflect subjects' behavior.

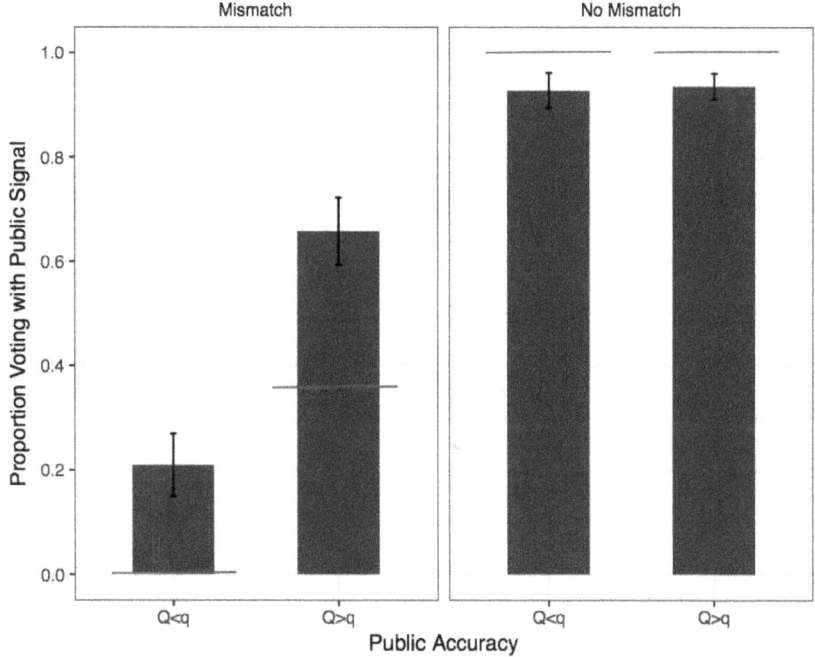

Figure 1. Responsiveness of vote to signals' precision: Average fraction of votes with public signal in sessions with committee decisions, and associated 95% confidence intervals. Standard errors are clustered at the individual level. In the left plot, the public signal and the private signal disagree, and red lines represent the symmetric responsive equilibrium prediction for μ, the probability of voting for the public signal under mismatch. In the right plot, the signals agree, and blue lines represent the unique optimal decision when the two signals agree.

---

[12] One possibility is that subjects realize that others do not play the symmetric responsive equilibrium, and best respond to that. For instance, if a subject realizes that some other committee members always play the conformist equilibrium in favor of the public signal, then she would best respond by voting for the public signal *less* than what prescribed by the symmetric responsive equilibrium. In each session, the average vote with the public signal (when signals do not match) is close to 60%. A best-response to this would be to vote with the public signal less than 37% of the time (the symmetric responsive equilibrium prediction). The data show that subjects follow the public signal more than what these best replies to experimental data predict.

The results in Figure 1 can be disaggregated to shed light on individual behavior.[13] Figure 2 plots the proportion of times each subject votes according to the public signal. We know that in the symmetric responsive equilibrium this proportion should be 37% when $Q > q$ and zero when $Q \leq q$ (when the public and private signals disagree). On the other hand, were people playing the conformist equilibrium, the proportion would be close to one for both values of signal precision. Figure 2 show these equilibrium predictions and subjects' deviations from them, which are bigger as the distance between the equilibrium predictions and the bars increase. This result again contradicts the coordination motive of players, as more subjects vote following the public signal when its precision is higher (upper graph) than when it is lower than the private one (lower graph).

One concern that could arise is that subjects' behavior changed over time, approaching the theoretical predictions of the equilibria analyzed. Figure A9 in Appendix A analyzes the dynamics of subjects' behavior over time, showing that there is no convergence to equilibrium predictions as the final rounds approach.

The next section describes how subjects responded to salience of public signals. According to the salience mechanism, framing leads subjects to select a strategy based on the frame itself, even if it is strategically irrelevant.

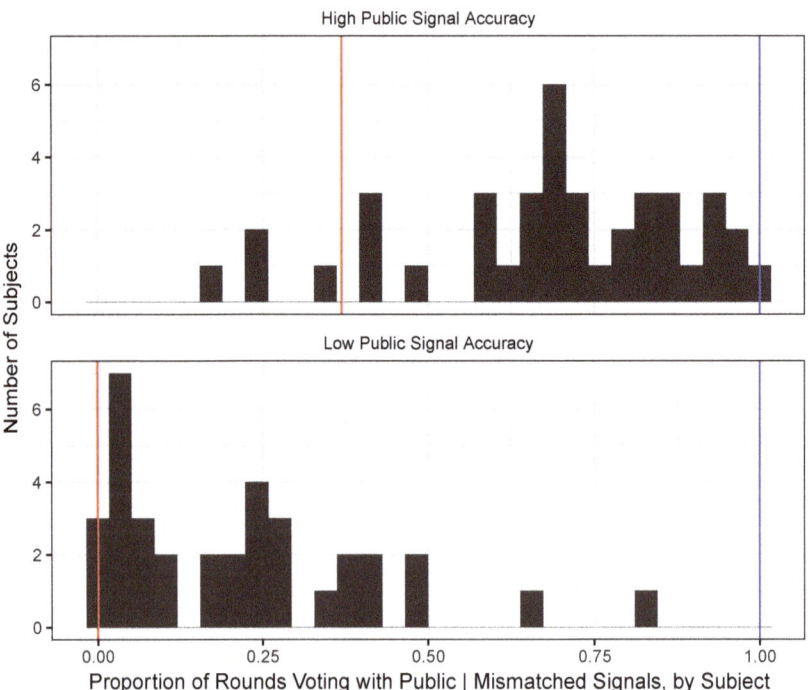

Figure 2. Individual deviations from equilibria under mismatch: Red lines represent the symmetric equilibrium predictions for μ, when the public and private signal disagree. Blue lines represent the conformist equilibrium prediction. When $Q > q$ (upper picture), the number of subjects who vote more with the public signal is greater than when $Q < q$ (lower picture).

---

[13] It might be that some subjects are playing the conformist equilibria and others are mixing. With Figure 1 we would not be able to disentangle between the two behaviors.

4.1. Subjects' Response to Salience

This section reports separately the results for each salience treatment, starting from the asymmetric prior, which is the treatment where the public message is least salient (as it is not displayed at all), and continuing with the more salient treatments (recency and jingle).

Asymmetric Prior. Figure 3 shows the proportion of votes with the public signal (under mismatch) in the treatment with public signal calculated by aggregating over the other salience treatments vs. the treatment with asymmetric prior.

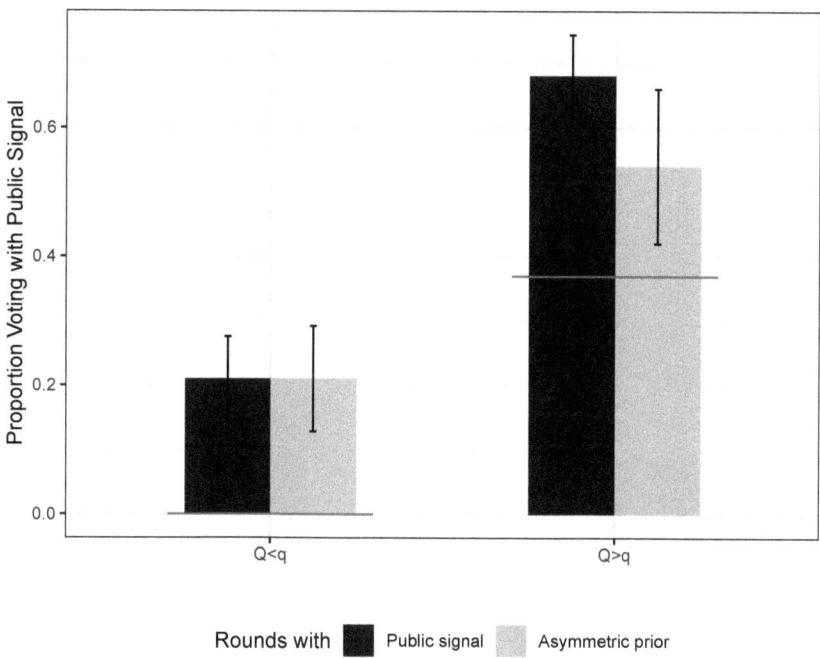

Figure 3. Asymmetric prior treatment: Average fraction of votes with public signal under mismatch, and 95% confidence intervals. Standard errors are clustered at the individual level. Dark columns correspond to rounds where the public signal was provided. Light columns correspond to the last 10 rounds in each sessions, where the public signal content was conflated into the prior. Note: Horizontal lines represent the symmetric responsive equilibrium prediction for μ.

The left bars correspond to the public signal being less accurate than the private ($Q < q$), and we see no difference. When $Q > q$ instead, subjects follow the public signal more (as we saw earlier), and the treatment effect of showing the public signal is high and significant: showing the public signal correlates with subjects voting for it 14% of the times more than when the same signal is conflated in the prior. This difference is significant at the ten percent level. This treatment effect has the same direction of what found in KV,[14] although the magnitude is much smaller. One concern might be that any effect of the asymmetric prior treatment is driven by it being administered during the last ten rounds of each session. I performed the same comparison as in Figure 3 considering only the last ten rounds of the first part of the experiment, when the public signal was displayed. Even with this

---

[14] KV only analyze the case where $Q > q$, with slightly different parameters and committee size.

reduced sample, there is no difference when the public signal is less precise. When the public signal is more precise, this difference is reduced to 11 percentage points, significant at the ten percent level.

Recency. The recency treatment varied whether the public signal was projected on the central screens of the laboratory before or after the private signals were displayed on the subjects' monitors. Recency effects were substantively and statistically significant. In particular, when the public signal accuracy is higher (right columns in Figure 4), there is a 16% difference between the fraction of times subjects followed the public signal when it was displayed before the private (60%) as opposed to after the private (76%). When the public signal accuracy is lower than the private (left columns), there is a 11% difference. Both differences are significant at any conventional level.

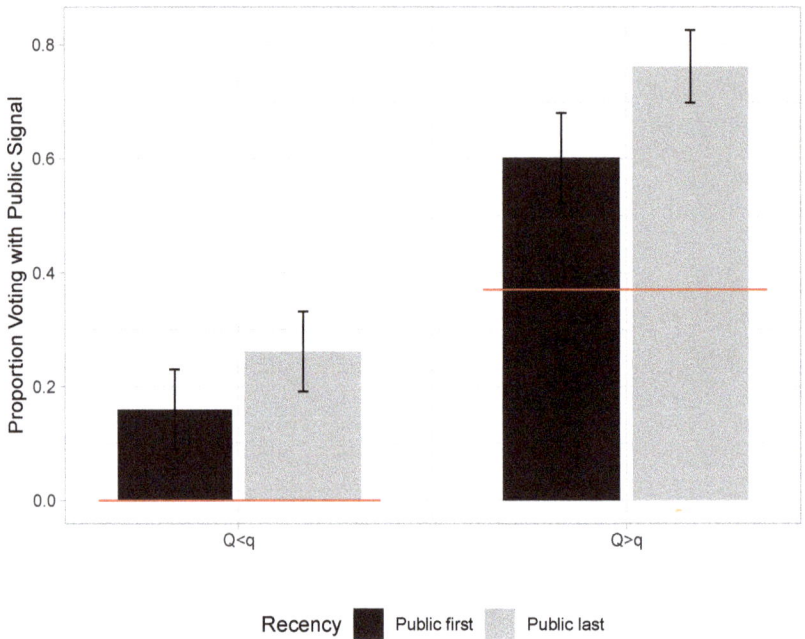

Figure 4. *Recency effect*: Average fraction of votes with public signal under mismatch, and 95% confidence intervals. Standard errors are clustered at the individual level. Dark columns correspond to rounds where the public signal is displayed first. Horizontal lines represent symmetric responsive equilibrium predictions for μ.

Jingle. For what concerns the jingle treatment effect, the direction is the one expected and it is in line with the recency treatment effect. The magnitude is smaller, as Figure 5 shows. When the public signal accuracy is higher (right columns in Figure 5), there is a 4% difference between the fraction of times subjects followed the public signal when it was displayed before the private (67%) as opposed to closer to the vote (71%). When the public signal accuracy is lower than the private (left columns), there is a 5% difference.

Table 3 shows an OLS regression of the probability of following the public signal under mismatch, regressed on the jingle treatment and the recency treatment. When the public signal is presented as a flashy video, subjects vote for it 4.7% of the time more. When we interact the jingle with recency, the effect increases to 5.9%. Even though the aggregate effect of the jingle is not significant, there is a pattern of response to it: subjects react more to the initial jingles. In particular, if the jingles are shown within the first 15 periods, subjects follow the public signal more than public signal displayed in later periods (12% difference, $p < 0.01$).

Given the magnitude and significance of the recency treatment effect, the question that arises is whether this effect is homogeneous across subjects. Figure 6 shows the individual treatment effect of recency of the public signal. Each dot represents the proportion of times each subject voted with the public signal. The vertical distance between red and blue dots is the individual average treatment effect of providing a public signal before vs. after the private one. The left panel corresponds to a more precise public signal. Recency of the public signal has a striking homogeneous, positive effect on the proportion of time each individual votes with the public signal.

We can see this effect from the proportion of times each individual voted with the public signal when it is displayed closer to the vote (dark dots), which is always above the same proportion when the public signal is displayed before the private signal (light dots): the "Public Last" (recency) treatment first order stochastically dominates the "Pubic First" treatment.[15]

Overall, there is a substantial fraction of subjects who always vote according to the most recent signal. In particular, votes match the most recent signal in 74% of individual decision, which is a remarkable result given that from a theoretical standpoint behavior should not be affected by the time a message is released. Moreover, subjects' behavior is homogeneous across different sessions.[16]

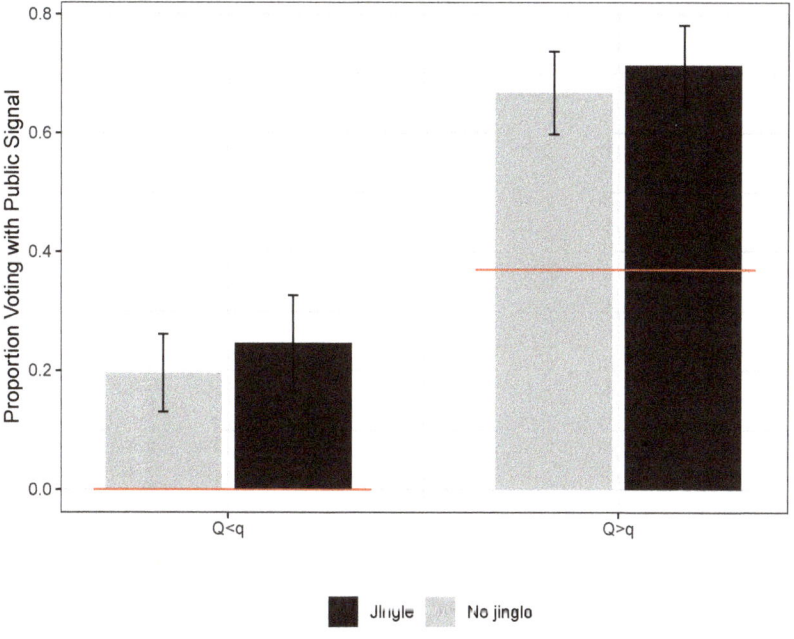

Figure 5. **Jingle effect**: Average fraction of votes with public signal under mismatch, and 95% confidence intervals. Standard errors are clustered at the individual level. Dark columns correspond to rounds where the public signal is displayed with the jingle. Horizontal lines represent symmetric responsive equilibrium predictions for μ.

---

[15] I also performed a Kolmogorov–Smirnov test to compare the two samples of voting for the public signal when it is provided before or after the private. Although we cannot reject that the two distribution are the same (with a p-value of 0.15), the number of observation is too small to rely on this result, and graphically showing the ECDFs provides much better evidence.
[16] As Figures A4 and A5 in Appendix A show, there are no session-specific effects: individual votes are homogeneous across different sessions.

Table 3. OLS regression. The dependent variable is a dummy variable equal to 1 when public and private signals differ, and the subject votes according to the public signal, 0 otherwise. The variable *Jingle* is a dummy variable equal to 1 when the public information is displayed with a salient video, and the variable *Public last* is a dummy variable equal to 1 when the public signal is displayed after the private signal. Column (3) shows that, when controlling for order effects, the effect of the jingle remains significant, but the magnitude of recency is higher. Standard errors are clustered at the individual level in parenthesis. * corresponds to $p < 0.1$ and *** to $p < 0.01$.

	Vote Public		
	(1)	(2)	(3)
Jingle	0.047 * (0.024)		0.059 * (0.034)
Public Last		0.131 *** (0.022)	0.138 *** (0.026)
Jingle * Public Last			−0.025 (0.049)
Observations	2068	2068	2068

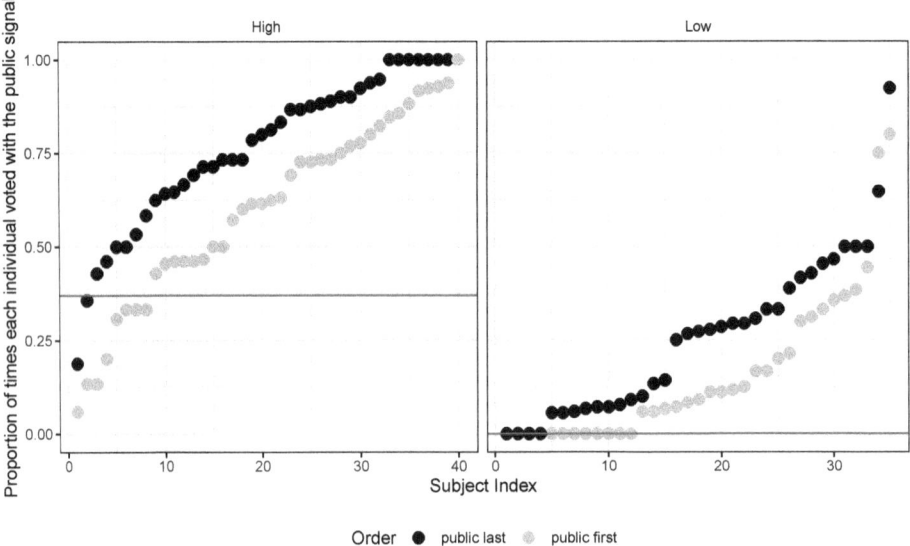

Figure 6. Individual average treatment effect of recency. Each dot represents the proportion of rounds an individual votes with the public signal under mismatch. Dark dots correspond to when the public signal is more recent, light dots when the private is more recent. Horizontal lines represent the symmetric responsive equilibrium predictions for μ. Recency has a positive, constant effect across different subjects.

4.2. Individual Treatment Sessions

In the previous section, I show that the way subjects responded to the signals' relative precision rules out the coordination mechanism, which is a possibility that might arise (see conformity equilibrium in the theory section). Sessions 5–10 were designed to fully control for this coordination mechanism. The structure of these sessions was identical to the previous four, except that subjects were paid for their individual decisions, and were not part of any group. Instructions were given to subjects in the same way as in the first sessions, with the only difference that no groups were mentioned.

The absence of groups made the decision much easier, being absent any calculus of pivotality or coordination problem. The decision problem was straightforward, as it only required to compare the relative precision of the signals received: the expected payoff maximizing decision was to always follow the information contained in the more accurate message.

If less subjects followed the public signal in these individual sessions, we would have evidence that subjects used the public signal as a coordination device: voters would conform to the public signal's content as long as they were in groups, but would stop to conform when the task was individual. If, on the other hand, the fractions of people voting for the public signal were similar in the individual and group treatments, it would be evidence that subjects did not use the public signal as a coordination device.

Aggregate data for these individual sessions show that there is no substantive difference between the fraction of votes cast according to the public signal in the individual task treatment versus the treatment with committees and group decisions (see Figure 7).

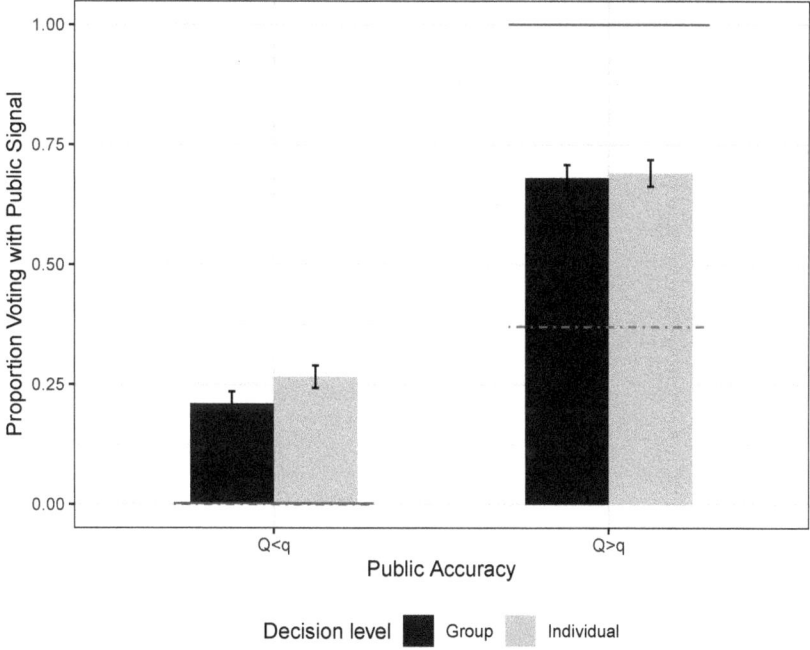

Figure 7. Individual task vs. group task. Average fraction of votes with public signal, with 95% confidence intervals. Standard errors are clustered at the individual level. Horizontal dotted lines represent symmetric responsive equilibrium predictions for μ. Solid lines represent the unique optimal decision in the individual treatment (follow the more precise signal).

The aggregate data show that, when the public signal is less precise than the private, subjects tend to over-follow the public (the optimal decision is to never vote with the public in both group and individual treatments). The treatment effect of relative signal precision remains in the correct direction even in the individual sessions. The similar results that we observe in the group task and individual task sessions provide evidence against the coordination mechanism in the group treatment. Yet, the fact that individuals vote too little with the public signal when it is more informative than the private is surprising, given the very simple task they are given. This result might be due to the way subjects were exposed to the messages during the experiment. Although preserving the same experimental design used in the first sessions with the group task was the most linear way to compare the two treatment conditions, some subjects might have been confused by receiving a public signal common to everyone in the room, when their payoff was determined uniquely by their decision. Hence, despite very clear instructions, the individual task might have confused some subjects. This confusion presumably did not arise in the group sessions, where the presence of a public signal observed by all subjects was intuitively related to group decision making.

As Figure 8 shows, individual data for the individual sessions show the same stochastic dominance that we saw in group sessions for the recency treatment. Even for these subjects, recency of the public signal has a homogeneous and positive effect on the proportion of time each individual votes with the public signal. We can see this effect from the distribution of individual votes when the public signal is displayed closer to the vote (dark dots), which stochastically dominates the votes when the public signal is displayed before the private (light dots). Even the jingle has an effect that is similar to the group sessions: when the public signal is presented as a flashy video with salient music, the probability that subjects vote for it is 5% higher (p-value lower than 10%), although when interacted with recency, this effect is not significant anymore (Table A1 in Appendix A shows the OLS regression coefficients for the individual sessions). Overall, the individual sessions show that salience treatment effects (particularly in the form of recency) are robust to the nature of the task: whether subjects vote in groups or individually, they are clearly affected by the way the message is presented.[17]

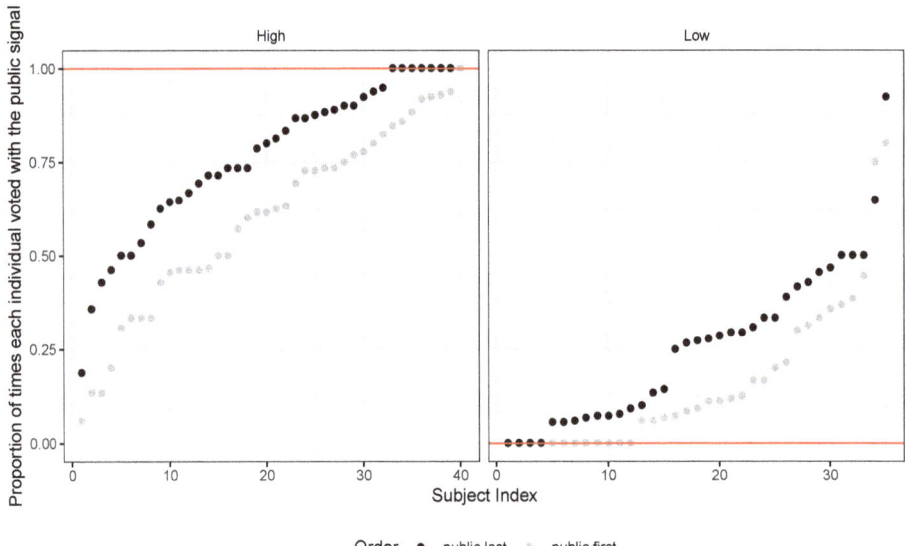

Figure 8. Recency effect (individual sessions). Each dot represents the proportion of rounds an individual votes with the public signal. Dark dots correspond to when the public signal is more recent, light dots when the private is more recent. The left image plots values for sessions where $Q > q$, the right one $Q < q$. Horizontal lines represent the symmetric responsive equilibrium predictions for μ. Recency has a positive, constant effect across different subjects.

5. Conclusions

This paper studies the effect of salient public signals on voting behavior in a majoritarian voting game with common interest. When (in addition to private independent signals) a public signal is

---

[17] All the salience treatment effects in the individual task sessions are shown in Appendix A.

observed by everyone, there exist two main equilibria of interest: a symmetric responsive equilibrium, where subjects follow their private signals with positive probability, and a Bayesian equilibrium where subjects coordinate on the information provided by the public signal. Theoretically, subjects' behavior should not be affected by signals' salience, as long as the informational content of the signals is the same.

A laboratory experiment tests these theoretical predictions, suggesting several conclusions. First, subjects tend to follow the public signal more than what is predicted by the symmetric responsive equilibrium. If subjects treated public signals as information devices, we would expect this result only for the treatment with high public signal accuracy ($Q > q$), as in Reference [11]. Yet, subjects tend to over follow the public signal even when it is less accurate than the private one, as Figure 1 shows. One might hypothesize that public signals are focal points acting as coordination devices when decisions are taken in groups. As shown in Figure 2, this mechanism is contradicted by the data. Moreover, results from the individual sessions disregard the coordination mechanism, as subjects vote very similarly whether they are in groups or not.

The second conclusion is that salience of information affects voter behavior. Different treatments investigate whether subjects follow the public signal because it is displayed in a salient manner. In particular, experimental results show that the order of message delivery matters, as subjects tend to follow the public signal more when it is the most recent signal observed before voting. Interestingly, this finding is robust to sessions where subjects do not vote in committees over issues of common interest. This result of recency effect mirrors what observed in field experiments on political message effectiveness during electoral campaigns [13].

The effect of recency of public information can have important political implications. Consider for instance the timing of political scandals' breaking: if the timing of message delivery matters, then it is more likely that voters take into account a scandal involving a politician when voting if the scandal happens close to the election date. A recent illustration of what is known as an "October surprise" in American Politics was Comey's announcement about reopening the email investigation of Hillary Clinton's emails. The announcement came on 28 October 2016, ten days before the Presidential election won by Donald Trump. Although it is hard to assess the effect of this announcement on the election's outcome, it is reasonable to believe that this affected voters more than had it been announced six months before. The fact that voters overreact to salient, recent information, can explain the strategic choice of when to drop a bombshell.

Funding: This research was funded by the Columbia Experimental Laboratory for the Social Sciences (CELSS).

Conflicts of Interest: The author declares no conflict of interest.

Appendix A. Online Appendix

Appendix A.1. Proofs—Preliminaries

Let's first consider for simplicity a committee of size $n = 3$. The next section generalizes to committees of arbitrary size. Define by μ the probability that a voter votes according to the public signal (in favor of state A), when her private signal is the opposite (in favor of state B), that is, $\mu = Pr(v_i = \alpha | s_i = \beta, s_p = \alpha)$.

Under pivotality, the posterior probabilities of state A and state B being true given signals $s_i = \alpha, s_p = \beta$ are respectively:

$$Pr[A|\alpha, \beta, piv] = \frac{Pr[s_i = \alpha|A]Pr[s_p = \beta|A]Pr[piv|A, s_i = \alpha, s_p = \beta]Pr(A)}{Pr[s_i = \alpha, s_p = \beta, piv|A] + Pr[s_i = \alpha, s_p = \beta, piv|B]}$$

$$= \frac{q(1-Q)q(1-\mu)[q\mu + (1-q)1]\pi}{q(1-Q)q(1-\mu)[q\mu + (1-q)1] + (1-q)Q(1-q)(1-\mu)[q1 + (1-q)\mu]}$$

$$Pr[B|\alpha,\beta,piv] = \frac{Pr[s_i=\alpha|B]Pr[s_p=\beta|B]Pr[piv|B,s_i=\alpha,s_p=\beta]Pr(B)}{Pr[s_i=\alpha,s_p=\beta,piv|A] + Pr[s_i=\alpha,s_p=\beta,piv|B]}$$

$$= \frac{(1-q)Q[(1-q)(1-\mu)][q1+(1-q)\mu]\pi}{q(1-Q)q(1-\mu)[q\mu+(1-q)1] + (1-q)Q(1-q)(1-\mu)[q1+(1-q)\mu]}$$

Player i votes for alternative A when receiving signals $s_i = \alpha$ and $s_p = \beta$ if

$$EU(v_i = A|s_i = \alpha, s_p = \beta, S_{-i}) \geq EU(v_i = B|s_i = \alpha, s_p = \beta, S_{-i})$$

With a normalized utility function, under pivotality:

$$EU(v_i = A|\alpha,\beta,piv) = \frac{q(1-Q)q(1-\mu)[q\mu+(1-q)1]\pi}{q(1-Q)q(1-\mu)[q\mu+(1-q)1] + (1-q)Q(1-q)(1-\mu)[q1+(1-q)\mu]} \quad (A1)$$

$$EU(v_i = B|\alpha,\beta,piv) = \frac{(1-q)Q[(1-q)(1-\mu)][q1+(1-q)\mu]\pi}{q(1-Q)q(1-\mu)[q\mu+(1-q)1] + (1-q)Q(1-q)(1-\mu)[q1+(1-q)\mu]}. \quad (A2)$$

Appendix A.2. Main Results

Proof of Lemma 1. We are looking for an equilibrium in which agents always follow the private signal when the public signal goes in the opposite direction: this corresponds to $\mu = 0$. For this value of μ, the pure strategy is to vote according to the private signal whenever its accuracy is greater than that of the public one.

Committee of size 3. To find the values of q, Q such that it is a dominant strategy to follow the private signal, set Equation (A1) equal to Equation (A2) and $\mu = 0$:

$$EU(v_i = A|s_i = 0, s_p = 1, pivot) = EU(v_i = B|s_i = 0, s_p = 1, pivot) \quad (A3)$$

$$q(1-Q) = (1-q)Q,$$

$$\frac{q}{1-q} = \frac{Q}{1-Q}$$

which shows that, when $q > Q$, it is a dominant strategy to follow the private signal.

Committee of arbitrary size. In this case, Equation (A3) becomes

$$EU(v_i = A|s_i = \alpha, s_p = \beta, pivot) = EU(v_i = B|s_i = \alpha, s_p = \beta, pivot)$$

$$\pi q(1-Q)\binom{N-1}{\frac{N-1}{2}}[(1-\mu)q]^{\frac{N-1}{2}}[\mu q]^{\frac{N-1}{2}} = \pi Q(1-q)\binom{N-1}{\frac{N-1}{2}}[1-\mu(1-q)]^{\frac{N-1}{2}}[\mu(1-q)]^{\frac{N-1}{2}}$$

$$q(1-Q)\binom{N-1}{\frac{N-1}{2}}[\mu q]^{\frac{N-1}{2}}[1-\mu q]^{\frac{N-1}{2}} = Q(1-q)\binom{N-1}{\frac{N-1}{2}}[\mu(1-q)]^{\frac{N-1}{2}}[(1-\mu(1-q)]^{\frac{N-1}{2}}$$

$$q(1-Q)[\mu q]^{\frac{N-1}{2}}[1-\mu q]^{\frac{N-1}{2}} = Q(1-q)[\mu(1-q)]^{\frac{N-1}{2}}[(1-\mu(1-q)]^{\frac{N-1}{2}}$$

Rearranging yields:

$$\frac{q}{(1-q)}\left(\frac{q/1-q}{Q/1-Q}\right)^{\frac{2}{N-1}}[1-(1-\mu)q] = 1 - (1-q)(1-\mu). \quad (A4)$$

Setting $\mu = 0$ we can simplify Equation (A5) as

$$\frac{q}{(1-q)}\left(\frac{q/1-q}{Q/1-Q}\right)^{\frac{2}{N-1}} = \frac{q}{(1-q)} \tag{A5}$$

which shows that, when $q > Q$, it is a dominant strategy to follow the private signal.

Hence, there exists an equilibrium in which every agent always vote with the private signal if and only if $Q \leq q$. In this equilibrium, agents never follow the public signal, that is, $\mu = 0$. □

Proof of Proposition 1. Committee of size 3. In order to characterize the equilibrium mixing probability, μ, we set equal the expected utilities for the two alternatives

$$EU(v_i = A|s_i = \alpha, s_p = \beta, piv) = EU(v_i = B|s_i = \alpha, s_p = \beta, piv)$$
$$q^2(1-Q)[1-q(1-\mu)] = (1-q)^2 Q[1-(1-\mu)(1-q)],$$
$$q^2(1-Q) - \mu q^3(1-Q) = (1-q)^2 Q - \mu(1-q)^3 Q$$
$$\mu[(1-q)^3 Q - q^3(1-Q)] = (1-q)^2 Q - q^2(1-Q).$$

which corresponds to the following value for the equilibrium probability of following the public signal

$$\mu = \frac{(q-1)q(q-Q)}{q^3 - 3(q-1)qQ - q}. \tag{A6}$$

In order to find the threshold Q^H, consider the case of $\mu = 1$. For this value of μ, the pure strategy is to vote according to the public signal whenever its accuracy is greater than the following value. In a committee of three members, this is equal to

$$EU(v_i = A|s_i = \alpha, s_p = \beta, piv) = EU(v_i = B|s_i = \alpha, s_p = \beta, piv)$$
$$\frac{(1-Q)}{Q} = \frac{(1-q)^2}{q^2}$$
$$\frac{1}{Q} - 1 = \frac{(1-2q+q^2)}{q^2}$$
$$\frac{1}{Q} = \frac{(1-2q+q^2+q^2)}{q^2}$$
$$Q^H = \frac{q^2}{(1-2q+2q^2)}.$$

Committee of arbitrary size. Consider a committee of arbitrary size N (with N odd). In order to characterize the equilibrium mixing probability, μ, set

$$EU(v_i = A|s_i = \alpha, s_p = \beta, pivot) = EU(v_i = B|s_i = \alpha, s_p = \beta, pivot)$$

$$\pi q(1-Q)\binom{N-1}{\frac{N-1}{2}}[(1-\mu)q]^{\frac{N-1}{2}}[\mu q]^{\frac{N-1}{2}} = \pi Q(1-q)\binom{N-1}{\frac{N-1}{2}}[1-\mu(1-q)]^{\frac{N-1}{2}}[\mu(1-q)]^{\frac{N-1}{2}}$$

$$q(1-Q)\binom{N-1}{\frac{N-1}{2}}[\mu q]^{\frac{N-1}{2}}[1-\mu q]^{\frac{N-1}{2}} = Q(1-q)\binom{N-1}{\frac{N-1}{2}}[\mu(1-q)]^{\frac{N-1}{2}}[(1-\mu(1-q)]^{\frac{N-1}{2}}$$

$$q(1-Q)[\mu q]^{\frac{N-1}{2}}[1-\mu q]^{\frac{N-1}{2}} = Q(1-q)[\mu(1-q)]^{\frac{N-1}{2}}[(1-\mu(1-q)]^{\frac{N-1}{2}}.$$

Rearranging we get the following:

$$\frac{q}{(1-q)}\left(\frac{q/1-q}{Q/1-Q}\right)^{\frac{2}{N-1}}\mu[1-q+q(1-\mu)] = [q-(1-q)(1-\mu)].$$

We want to solve for μ. Let us call γ the following value

$$\frac{q}{(1-q)}\left(\frac{q/1-q}{Q/1-Q}\right)^{\frac{2}{N-1}} \quad (A7)$$

which allows to rewrite the previous equation as

$$\gamma[1-(1-\mu)q] = 1-(1-q)(1-\mu) \quad (A8)$$

Solving for μ, we get

$$\mu = \frac{\gamma - q(1+\gamma)}{1-q-q\gamma}, \quad (A9)$$

Therefore, in a committee of arbitrary size, the agents whose private signal disagrees with the public vote according to the private with probability $\mu = \frac{\gamma-q(1+\gamma)}{1-q-q\gamma}$, where $\gamma(q,Q,N) = \left(\frac{q/1-q}{Q/1-Q}\right)^{\frac{2}{N-1}} \frac{q}{(1-q)}$. A proof of uniqueness is provided by Reference [15] and KV. □

Proof of Corollary 1. This follows from Proposition 1, substituting $\mu = 1$. □

Appendix A.3. Aggregate Data—Individual Sessions

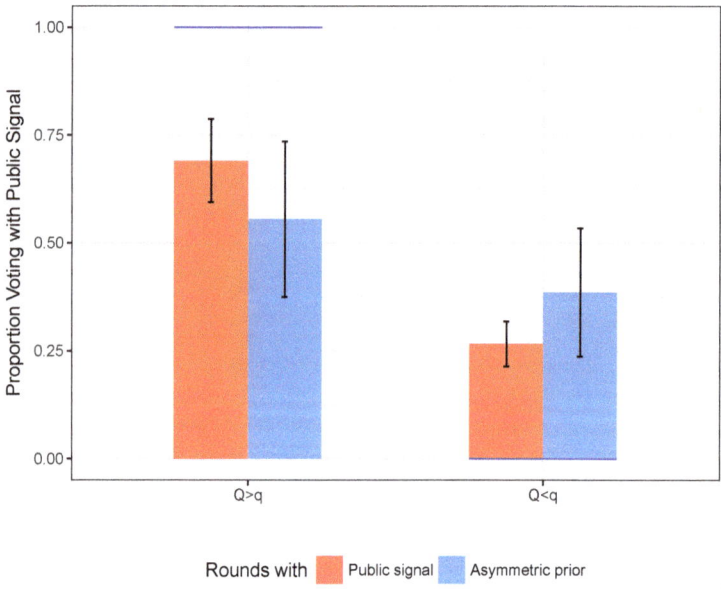

Figure A1. Asymmetric prior treatment in individual sessions. Average fraction of votes with public signal under mismatch and 95% confidence intervals. Standard errors are clustered at the individual level. The blue columns correspond to the last 10 rounds in each sessions, where the public signal content was conflated in the prior. Note: Blue lines represent the unique optimal decision in the individual treatment (follow the more precise signal).

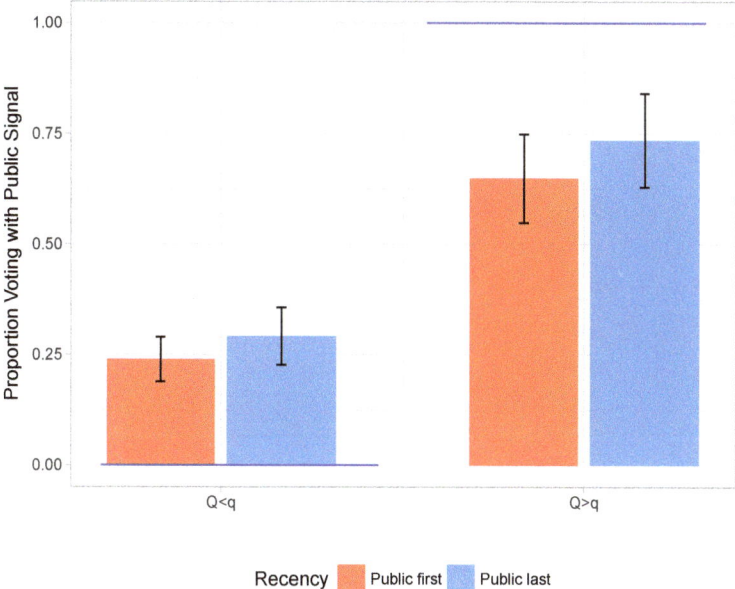

Figure A2. Recency effects in individual sessions. Average fraction of votes with public signal under mismatch and 95% confidence intervals. Standard errors are clustered at the individual level. Blue lines represent the unique optimal decision in the individual treatment (follow the more precise signal).

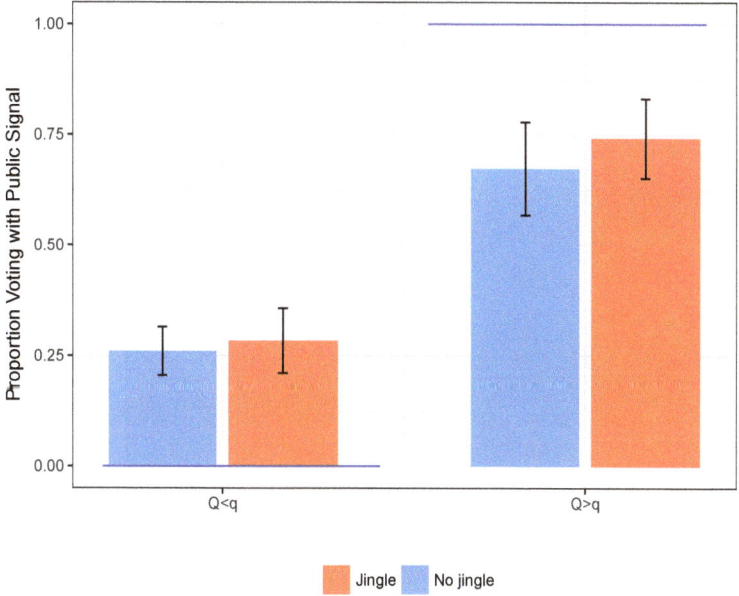

Figure A3. Jingle effects in individual sessions. Average fraction of votes with public signal under mismatch and 95% confidence intervals. Standard errors are clustered at the individual level. Blue lines represent the unique optimal decision in the individual treatment (follow the more precise signal).

Table A1. Jingle and recency effects in individual sessions. The dependent variable is a dummy variable equal to 1 when public and private signals differ, and the subject votes according to the public signal, 0 otherwise. The variable *Jingle* is a dummy variable equal to 1 when the public information is displayed with a salient video, and the variable *Public last* is a dummy variable equal to 1 when the public signal is displayed before the private signal. Column (3) shows that when controlling for order effects, the effect of the jingle is not significant anymore. Standard errors are clustered at the individual level in parenthesis. * corresponds to $p < 0.1$, ** to $p < 0.05$, and *** to $p < 0.01$.

	Vote Public		
	(1)	(2)	(3)
Jingle	0.048 **		0.050
	(0.023)		(0.033)
Public Last		0.055 ***	0.057 **
		(0.020)	(0.023)
Jingle * Public Last			−0.005
			(0.047)
Observations	2414	2414	2414

Appendix A.4. Individual Data

For the individual analysis, I first consider subjects in session 1 through 4, those with committees and a group decision making problem. Figure A4 clearly shows that subjects are homogeneous across different sessions. The plots indicate the proportion of times that each individual voted according to the private signal. The left image is for the sessions with higher public signal accuracy ($Q > q$), and the right one for the others ($q < Q$). Figure A5 performs the same check for the sessions with an individual task. There is no evidence that subjects respond heterogeneously to the public accuracy treatment.

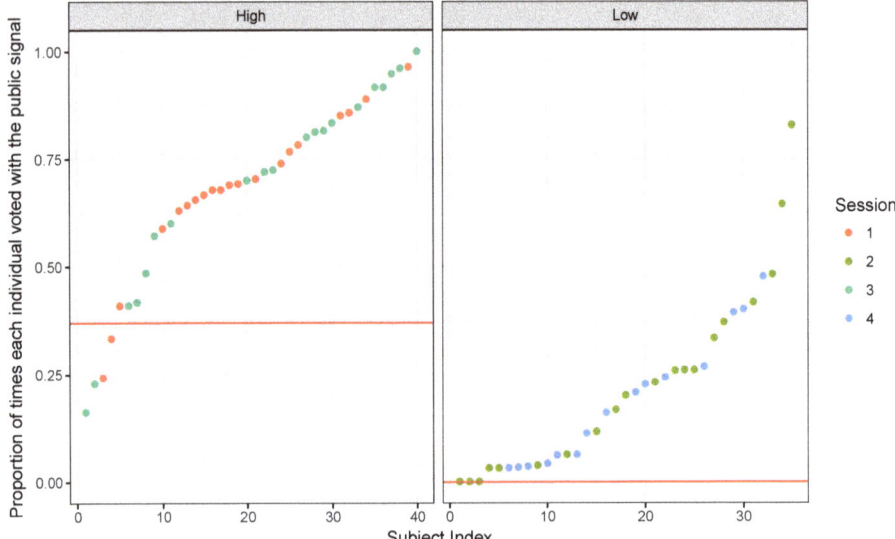

Figure A4. Proportion of times each individual voted according to the public signal in the first four sessions (with group task). The left image plots values for sessions where $Q > q$, the right one $Q < q$. Different colors correspond to different sessions.

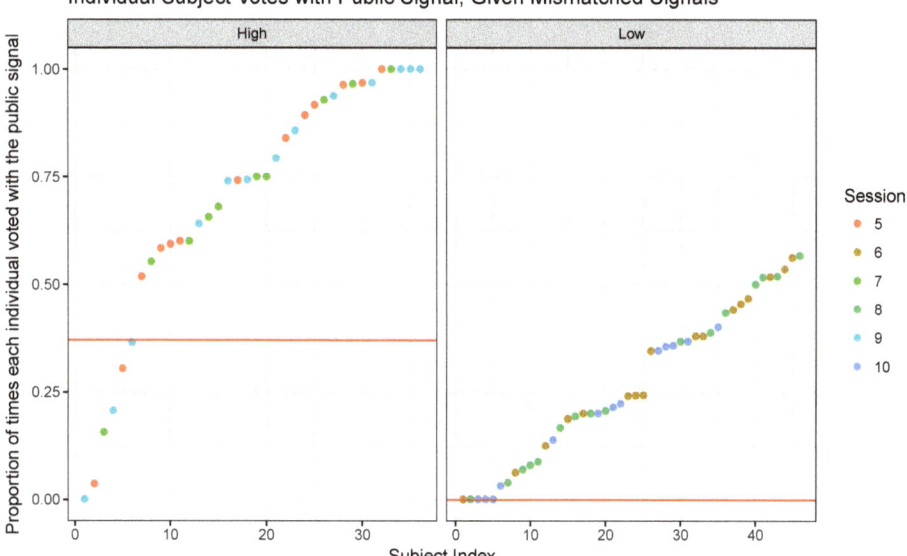

Figure A5. Proportion of times each individual voted according to the public signal in sessions 5–10 (with individual task). The left image plots values for sessions where $Q > q$, the right one $Q < q$. Different colors correspond to different sessions.

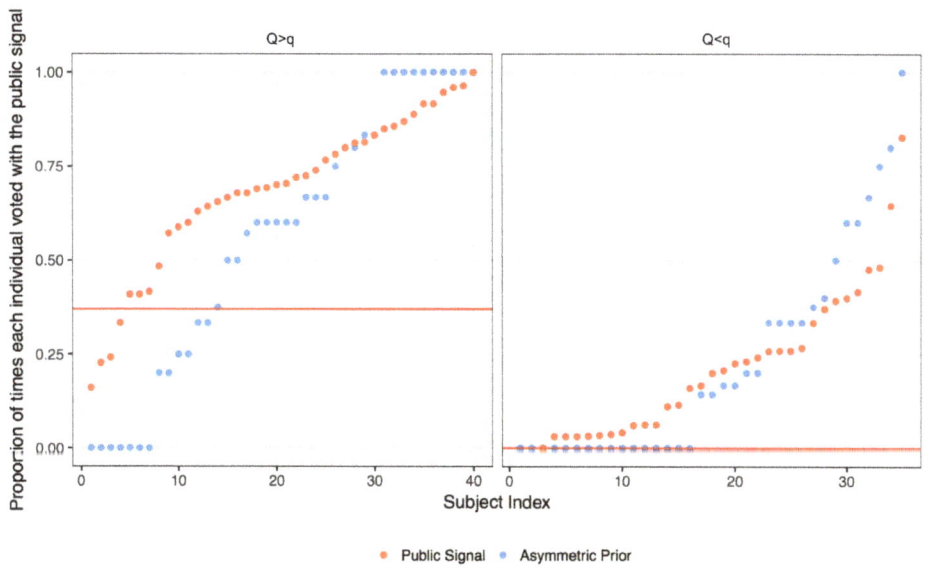

Figure A6. Asymmetric Prior (group task): Proportion of times each individual voted according to the public signal. The left image plots values for sessions where $Q > q$, the right one $Q < q$. Red dots correspond to the public signal delivered, blue dots to public signal conflated in the prior.

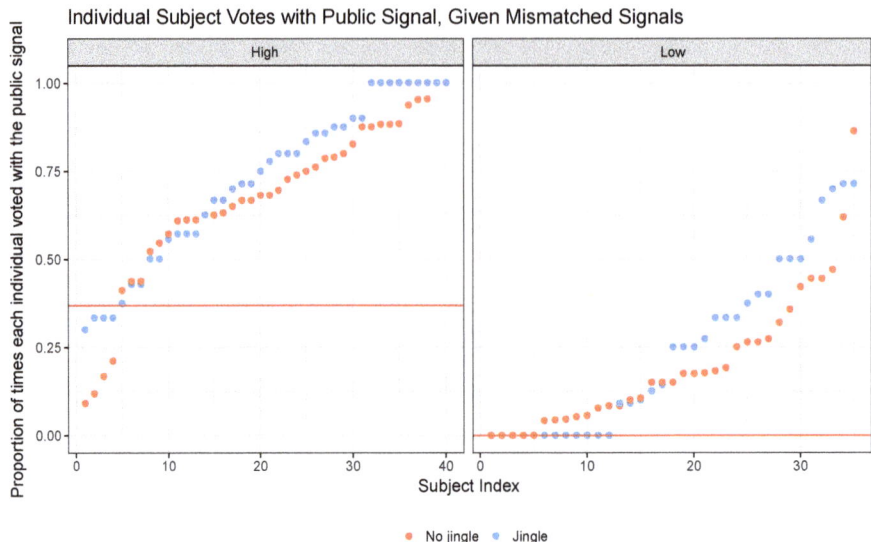

Figure A7. Jingle effect (group sessions). Proportion of times each individual voted according to the public signal. The left image plots values for sessions where $Q > q$, the right one $Q < q$. Blue dots correspond to the public signal displayed with the jingle.

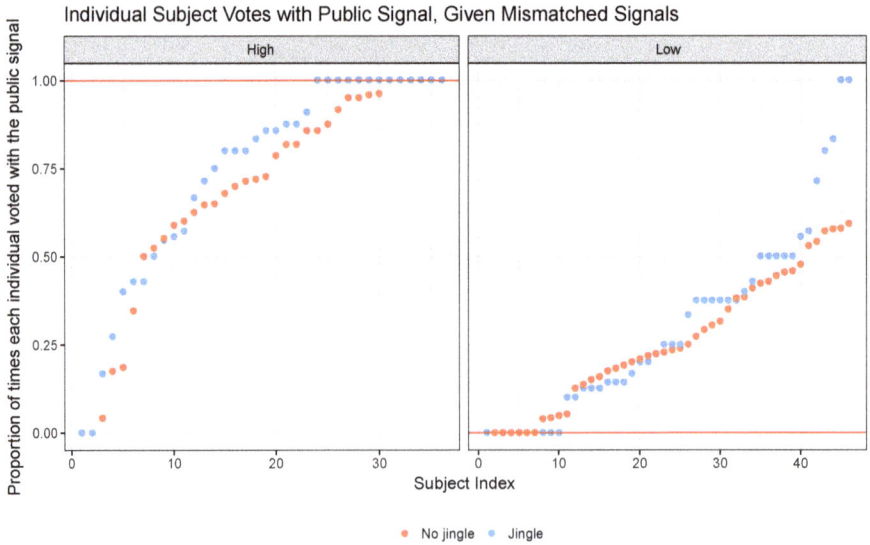

Figure A8. Jingle effect (individual sessions). Proportion of times each individual voted according to the publice signal. The left image plots values for sessions where $Q > q$, the right one $Q < q$. Blue dots correspond to the public signal displayed with the jingle.

Recall that each session is comprised of 70 rounds, and in the last ten rounds subjects received an asymmetric prior and no public signal. The information conveyed was the same. Figure A6 plots, for the group treatment, the difference in how individuals vote when they receive two separate signals, a private and a public (first 60 sessions), and when they only receive a private, and the public information is conveyed by the prior (last ten rounds). This treatment tests the null hypothesis that individuals behave as Bayesian in recognizing that the posterior is the same in the two cases. As we can see there is a lot of heterogeneity, which leads us to reject the null hypothesis of constant treatment effect among our subjects. The same robustness check is run for the recency and jingle treatments, and is displayed in the figures that follow.

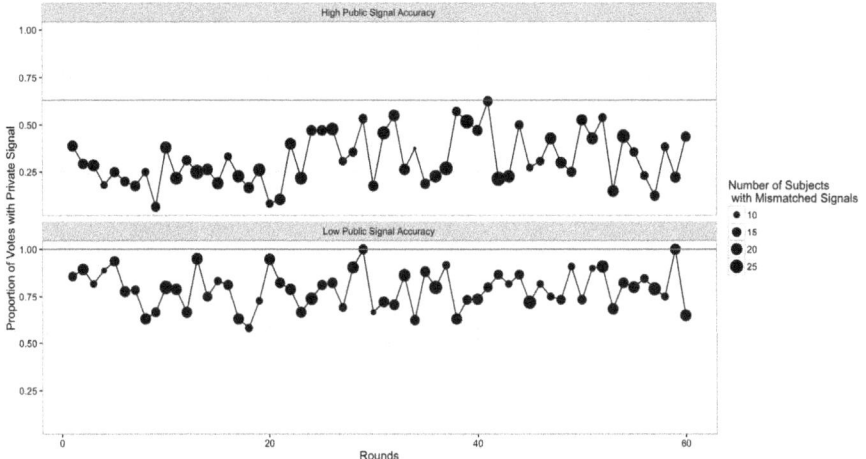

Figure A9. No Learning. This figure plot aggregate votes as a function of time (experimental rounds. Subjects' behavior does not approach theoretical predictions.)

Appendix A.5. Experimental Instructions

Welcome to the Lab![18] Please, listen to these instructions carefully. If you have any question at any point, please raise your hand. Communication between participants is not allowed during the experiment.

Your participation to the experiment will be rewarded by a payment in cash, immediately and privately after the experiment. The amount of money that you will earn depends on your decisions, the decisions of other participants, and on luck. During the experiment, your earnings will be calculated in experimental currency. After the experiment, your payoff will be converted into dollars (USD) according to the following conversion rate: 200 experimental dollars = 1 US dollar, rounded to the closest integer value. Additionally, you will receive 5 US dollars as a show-up fee, independently of the results during the experiment.

The experiment is comprised of two parts. The first part consists of a total of 60 rounds. The second part consists of a total of 10 rounds. During the first part, in every round you will be randomly divided in groups of five people. All participants are anonymous; nobody knows which other participants are in their group, and nobody will be told who was in which group after the experiment. Each group will make the same decisions, but what happens in the other groups has no relevance for yours. At the end of each round, the groups are newly shuffled.

At the beginning of each round, the computer places a prize in one of two virtual boxes: the blue box or the red box [SHOW PICTURE 1]. It is equally likely that the prize is placed in either box. You will not know which box the computer has chosen. Each group's task will be to guess which box contains the prize.

---

[18] These are the instructions for sessions with group task and high public signal accuracy. The other instructions and the pictures displayed during the instruction period are available upon request.

Each participant will receive two separate messages about the location of the prize. One message is private and only you can see it. The other message is public and everyone sees it.

The private message you receive is more likely to be correct than not, but it's not perfectly reliable. It is correct on average 60% of the times. The message is generated by the computer independently for each group member and revealed to each member separately. Private messages can be different for different group members.

In addition to the private message everyone receives, a public message will appear on the central screens. Is it correct on average 60% of the time. The public message may appear in different ways but *its accuracy does not depend on the format it takes* [emphasize].

Neither the public message nor the private messages are 100% reliable in predicting which box contains the prize, but both messages are more likely to be correct than incorrect. Consider the table on the screen: If the box selected by the computer is the red one, it is more likely that both messages are correct than not, and the least likely event is that both are wrong. [Picture 2].

After you and every member of your group have received both messages, you will be asked to guess which box contains the prize. You have two options: you can either vote for BLUE or for RED [SHOW PICTURE 3].

Remember that what matters for your earnings is the group decision. The box that receives the majority of the votes in your group of 5 people is the group choice for the round. In every round, each member of the group earns:

- 70 experimental dollars if the group guessed the correct box;
- 10 experimental dollars if the group guessed the wrong box.

Your earnings are determined exclusively by the group choice. These earnings are independent of how a particular group member voted.

At the end of the round you will learn:

1. The number of votes for the blue box cast by your group;
2. The number of votes for the red box cast by your group;
3. The box selected by majority in your group;
4. The outcome of the period: that is, whether the group decision was correct or not;
5. The earnings for the round.

[screenshot feedback screen]

This feedback screen marks the end of the round. After everyone votes, you will move to the next round, in which new groups are formed randomly. The prize is again randomly placed in one of the two boxes, and each box is equally likely to be selected.

In order to begin the experiment, you need to correctly answer to a brief questionnaire. If you have any question, ask now or during the questionnaire. When all the participants have completed the questionnaire, the first round of the experiment will automatically start.

Appendix A.6. Last Ten Rounds

Now that the first part of the experiment ended, you will start the second part, which is comprised of ten rounds.

As in part 1, at the beginning of each round, the computer places a prize in one of two virtual boxes: the blue box or the red box. Differently from the first part, in these rounds the computer places the prize in the BLUE box 7 out of 10 times, which means 70%. [slide: THE PRIZE IS PLACED IN BLUE BOX 7 OUT OF 10 TIMES]. The box that does not contain the prize remains empty. You will not know which box the computer has chosen. As in the previous part, the group's task will be to guess which box contains the prize.

In this part of the experiment, you will receive only a private message about the location of the prize. The private message you receive is more likely to be correct than not, but it's not perfectly reliable. It is correct on average 6 out of 10 times, which means 60%. The message is generated by the computer independently for each group member and revealed to each member separately. Private messages can be different for different group members. No other participant of the experiment will know which private message you received.

After you and every member of your group have received a message, you will be asked to guess which box contains the prize. As in part 1, you will see a feedback screen at the end of each round. If there are no question, you can now begin part 2.

We have now completed the experiment. Please, remain seated and wait for your number to be called and receive your payment.

References

1. Garthwaite, C.; Moore, T.J. Can celebrity endorsements affect political outcomes? Evidence from the 2008 US democratic presidential primary. *J. Law Econ. Organ.* **2012**, *29*, 355–384. [CrossRef]
2. Bordalo, P.; Gennaioli, N.; Shleifer, A. Salience theory of choice under risk. *Q. J. Econ.* **2012**, *127*, 1243–1285. [CrossRef]
3. Kahneman, D.; Tversky, A. Choices, values, and frames. *Am. Psychol.* **1984**, *39*, 341. [CrossRef]
4. Erev, I.; Haruvy, E. Learning and the economics of small decisions. In *The Handbook of Experimental Economics*; Princeton University Press: Princeton, NJ, USA, 2013; Volume 2, ISBN 9781400883172-011.
5. Fudenberg, D.; Peysakhovich, A. Recency, records, and recaps: Learning and nonequilibrium behavior in a simple decision problem. *ACM Trans. Econ. Comput. (TEAC)* **2016**, *4*, 23. [CrossRef]
6. Fudenberg, D.; Levine, D.K. Recency, consistent learning, and Nash equilibrium. *Proc. Natl. Acad. Sci. USA* **2014**, *111*, 10826–10829. [CrossRef] [PubMed]
7. Neligh, N. *Rational Memory with Decay*, 2019; unpublished work.
8. Strömberg, D. Media and politics. *Economics* **2015**, *7*, 173–205. [CrossRef]
9. Condorcet. *Essai sur L'application de L'analyse ala Probabilité des Décisions Rendues ala Pluralité des Voix (Essay on the Application of the Analysis to the Probability of Majority Decisions)*; L'Impremerie Royale: Paris, France, 1785; Facsimile edition New York: Chelsea, 1972.
10. Austen-Smith, D.; Banks, J.S. Information aggregation, rationality, and the Condorcet jury theorem. *Am. Political Sci. Rev.* **1996**, *90*, 34–45. [CrossRef]
11. Kawamura, K.; Vlaseros, V. Expert information and majority decisions. *J. Public Econ.* **2017**, *147*, 77–88. [CrossRef]
12. Gratton, G.; Holden, R.; Kolotilin, A. When to drop a bombshell. *Rev. Econ. Stud.* **2017**, *85*, 2139–2172. [CrossRef]
13. Nickerson, D.W. Quality is job one: Professional and volunteer voter mobilization calls. *Am. J. Political Sci.* **2007**, *51*, 269–282. [CrossRef]
14. Panagopoulos, C. Timing is everything? primacy and recency effects in voter mobilization campaigns. *Political Behav.* **2011**, *33*, 79–93. [CrossRef]
15. Wit, J. Rational choice and the Condorcet jury theorem. *Games Econ. Behav.* **1998**, *22*, 364–376. [CrossRef]
16. Liu, S. Voting with public information. *Games Econ. Behav.* **2019**, *113*, 694–719. [CrossRef]
17. Fischbacher, U. z-Tree: Zurich toolbox for ready-made economic experiments. *Exp. Econ.* **2007**, *10*, 171–178. [CrossRef]
18. Ciccarelli, S.K.; White, J.N.; Fritzley, V.H.; Harrigan, T. *Psychology: An Exploration*; Pearson Prentice Hall: Upper Saddle River, NJ, USA, 2010.
19. Crowder, R.G. *Principles of Learning and Memory: Classic Edition*; Psychology Press: New York, NY, USA; London, UK, 2014.
20. Cook, T.D.; Flay, B.R. The persistence of experimentally induced attitude change. *Adv. Exp. Soc. Psychol.* **1978**, *11*, 1–57.
21. Tversky, A.; Kahneman, D. Judgment under uncertainty: Heuristics and biases. *Science* **1974**, *185*, 1124–1131. [CrossRef] [PubMed]

© 2020 by the authors. Licensee MDPI, Basel, Switzerland. This article is an open access article distributed under the terms and conditions of the Creative Commons Attribution (CC BY) license (http://creativecommons.org/licenses/by/4.0/).

Article

Electoral Competition with Strategic Disclosure

Jacopo Bizzotto [1] and Benjamin Solow [2,*

1. Oslo Business School, Oslo Metropolitan University, 0166 Oslo, Norway; jacopo.bizzotto@oslomet.no
2. Department of Economics, University of Iowa, Iowa City, IA 52242, USA
* Correspondence: benjamin-solow@uiowa.edu; Tel.: +1-319-384-1911

Received: 30 April 2019; Accepted: 28 June 2019; Published: 6 July 2019

Abstract: Recent developments in information and communication technologies allow candidates for office to engage in sophisticated messaging strategies to influence voter choice. We consider how access to different technologies influence the choice of policy platforms by candidates. We find that when candidates can target messages to specific voter groups, platforms are more likely to be inefficient. In particular, when candidates can run targeted campaigns, they commit to projects that benefit small groups even when the social cost of these projects outweigh their benefits. Our results are robust to negative advertising.

Keywords: electoral competition; multidimensional policy space; microtargeting; office-motivated candidates; negative campaigning; strategic disclosure

JEL Classification: D72; D83; M37

---

1. Introduction

The advent of widespread internet use and rapidly improving computing power have fundamentally changed the tools available to advertisers. The 2018 Politics Issue of the MIT Technology Review illustrates how candidates in the last three US presidential races have used some of the same tools to reach the right voters with the right messages.[1] While candidates have always tailored campaign rhetoric to different groups, the scope for targeting has grown dramatically in recent years.[2] Political consulting companies, such as Catalist and CampaignGrid, have developed databases that include hundreds of millions of voters.[3] "Psychographic" advertising techniques exploit detailed data on individual preferences and lifestyle to improve targeting beyond demographics. Originally developed for commercial uses, these techniques have recently been adapted for electoral purposes.[4] This paper investigates how improvements in message targeting by candidates influence political competition.

We study a model in which two office-motivated candidates choose platforms and messages. Our model can be interpreted as describing voters divided into N interest groups, each seeking a

---

1. See "US election campaign technology from 2008 to 2018, and beyond" by A. Howard.
2. Gentzkow and Shapiro [1] document that online media has significantly larger ideological segregation than other forms of political information transmission. For an example of "traditional" ways to reach specific parts of the electorate, see the analysis of TV campaign ads during the 2000, 2004 and 2008 US presidential races in Ridout et al. [2].
3. On its website, Catalist advertises a database of approximately 240 million unique current voting-age individuals. CampaignGrid reports a database of more than 200 million voter profiles. For a general overview of data available for electoral campaigns in the US and Canada, see Bennet [3], for the UK see Anstead [4], for India see the article "Why India has nothing to fear from rightful use of big data" (*The Economic Times*, April 01, 2018).
4. Goldfarb and Tucker [5], Section 6.1, review the recent literature on personalized advertising. The article from *The Economic Times* mentioned in footnote 3, as well as the issue of the MIT Technology Review mentioned above summarize the state of the art (as of 2018) for advertising techniques used in electoral campaigns.

specific public good to be financed with national taxation. A platform can target any of those N groups by committing to provide the desired public good. Alternatively, a candidate can opt for a platform that does not promise any public good.

Our major departure from canonical models of targeting in politics [6,7] is to consider voters that are not perfectly informed about platforms even when those platforms may target their interests. We model voters as being either *informed* or *uninformed* about platforms. Informed voters observe all components of the chosen platforms. Uninformed voters, however, must rely on (truthful) messages from candidates. Uninformed voters receive a message from each candidate and each message reports whether the candidate has committed to provide a particular public good, or has committed not to provide that particular good.

We first consider a benchmark scenario in which all voters are informed, and show that candidates commit to whichever platform is socially efficient. We then consider three games that differ in the degree to which candidates can control their messages. These games correspond to different levels of sophistication in communication technologies. We first consider random messages. When messages are beyond the candidates' control, candidates commit to socially efficient platforms, as in the full-information benchmark. We then consider issue selection, i.e., we let each candidate control which message about his platform reaches the voters, yet all voters must receive the same message. In this game, candidates commit to efficient platforms as long as some voters are informed.

Finally, we consider microtargeting. We model microtargeting as candidates having the ability to target different groups of voters with different messages. We show that as long as the fraction of informed voters is not too large, equilibria in which all candidates commit to socially inefficient platforms exist. Furthermore, if informed voters are sufficiently rare, all equilibria are of this nature. Our main contribution is thus to highlight how message targeting can lead to inefficiencies in political platforms.

With microtargeted messages, inefficiencies arise when both of the following conditions hold. First, providing any public good is inefficient, so the unique efficient platform does not promise any public good. Second, informed voters are rare. When providing public goods is inefficient, the efficient platform does not promise any public good and ensures more votes from informed voters than any other platform. Doing so is costly, however, in that it forgoes sending targeted messages to uninformed voters who benefit from a specific public good. Promising a public good and targeting messages in this way increases the candidate's vote share among uninformed voters compared to choosing the platform that does not promise any public good. Thus, if sufficiently few voters are informed, none of the candidates commit to the efficient platform.

When efficient equilibria do not exist, there exist instead equilibria in which all candidates commit to provide a public good. In these equilibria candidates would benefit from deviating to the efficient platform if they could credibly communicate their deviation to all voters. Since messages are unidimensional, and different voters can be targeted with different messages, candidates cannot credibly communicate such a deviation if, for example, voters are skeptical and interpret any message reporting that some public good is not being financed as a signal that some other public good is being financed. Thus, the ability to fine tune political messages can, somewhat paradoxically, make it harder to communicate with voters.

We extend the model to show that this conclusion is robust to both limits on the targetability of platforms and negative advertising. When we restrict the targetability of platforms, but not messages, the qualitative results are unchanged. We model negative advertising by allowing one candidate to reveal the other candidate's platform. While efficient equilibria always exist under negative advertising, so too do inefficient equilibria for some parameter values.

While our model emphasizes simple messages, our results are also robust to relatively complex messages. The key restriction on message complexity is that candidates cannot perfectly reveal their entire platform to voters. In this sense, our study of communication technologies focuses on segmented media consumption rather than increasingly complex campaigning. While widespread internet media consumption does increase availability of complex information, it is widely recognized that even highly skilled and motivated agents fail to process all available information [8,9]. Indeed, this appears to be the case for voters as well [10]. One possible explanation is that in reality, the policy space has a large number of dimensions and it is potentially hard for voters to predict many issues on which the policymaker will be asked to make a decision while in office. Even given the opportunity, it is unlikely voters would choose to inform themselves on the minutiae of every dimension of policy space [11].

Our results suggest that providing additional flexibility in how candidates target messages to voters may harm the performance of the electoral system. In particular, our model suggests that the combination of detailed voter data and segregation of media consumption due to social media can erode the incentives for candidates to choose efficient policies. While we do not explicitly model the media, our model suggests that media competition, insofar as it segments the market even further, encourages inefficient outcomes of political competition.

The concern that better targeting of political messages might distort the choice of electoral platforms is discussed informally in Elmendorf and Wood [12]. Political microtargeting has also raised distinct and somewhat complementary concerns. First, as the Cambridge Analytica scandal has highlighted, voters' data could be collected in ways that violate individuals' privacy.[5] Furthermore, voters could be manipulated by candidates making false claims (see, for example, [13]). In the language of the economics of advertising, we focus on the informative content of political ads, while concerns over false claims or fake news are closely related to the persuasive role of these messages. Bagwell [14] describes the distinction between informative and persuasive views of advertising.

We discuss the related literature in Section 2. We describe the baseline model in Section 3, and analyze it in Section 4. Section 5 extends the model to include limited policy targetability and negative advertising. Section 6 concludes. The Appendix contains the proofs of the results that are not proved in the text.

2. Relevant Literature

Two strands of literature relate most closely to our paper. One literature considers the role of media and information transmission in politics. The other literature concerns itself with policy targeting, and more specifically with the tradeoff that candidates face between more easily targeted (inefficient) policies and broader (efficient) public goods projects. We discuss these two pieces of literature in turn.

The notion that voters are not perfectly informed is not controversial. Several papers have developed theories of political competition when voters have inaccurate perceptions of candidates' policy positions. The most similar paper to ours is Schipper and Woo [15]. Like us, they consider a game where candidates send messages to voters revealing portions of their multidimensional policy platform. They also consider different messaging technologies which correspond to what we call issue selection and microtargeting. A major difference with our work is that they consider exogenous platforms. Moreover, in their model, electoral competition with microtargeting is equivalent to electoral competition with full information. In our model, microtargeting may result in inefficient equilibria, whereas under full information, equilibria are always efficient. The difference in conclusions is due to message sophistication. While we allow microtargeting in the sense of sending a separate message to each voter, we do not let candidates send complex messages revealing their positions on multiple public goods.

Gratton et al. [16] also consider the question of strategic information revelation by candidates for office. In their model, candidates are vertically differentiated and choose when, if ever, to reveal their

---

[5] On March 17, 2018, *The Guardian* and *The New York Times* described the process by which Cambridge Analytica collected detailed data on individual voters through use of a Facebook app: "How Trump Consultants Exploited the Facebook Data of Millions" and "Revealed: 50 million Facebook profiles harvested for Cambridge Analytica in major data breach".

type to voters. The main concern is a tradeoff between credibility and scrutiny: high-quality candidates disclose information earlier in expectation, but this allows more time for voters to learn more about the disclosure. Our model differs in two ways. We study horizontal competition between candidates of equal quality and all information revealed is immediately verifiable costlessly. Nevertheless, we share the broad interest in strategic information disclosure when this disclosure may not be fully revealing.

Tyson [11] considers a model where a subset of voters are uninformed about a state variable that determines what the efficient policy is. He studies the decision of voters to become informed and turn out to vote, but leaves their set of alternatives fixed. Instead, in our model access to information is beyond the control of voters and we focus on which choices politicians will make in terms of both policy and information disclosure.

Ogden [17] analyzes platform choice by politicians who are competing in a Hotelling-Downs setting where voters observe platforms with noise. His main result is that platforms diverge unless observed without error. Similarly, in our model, platforms are efficient if they are observed by a large enough fraction of voters. We differ by studying a multidimensional issue space and considering different messaging technologies instead of the degree of noise around platform observation.

Aragonès et al. [18] study a model of issue selection featuring endogenous platforms. In their model, candidates invest in both platform quality and issue-specific advertising. As we consider issue selection in the sense of politicians sending all voters the same message, our model relies on horizontal rather than vertical competition. Our results under the issue selection technology align most closely with what they term the "homogenization effect" and positive issue races where candidates compete to provide extremely high-quality platforms. Demange and Van der Straeten [19] study a model at the intersection of Ogden [17] and Aragonès et al. [18] where investment in an issue reduces noise about the policy platform, and platforms are exogenous.

The second strand of literature concerns itself with policy targeting in models of redistributive politics. Conventional wisdom holds that politicians target resources towards groups of voters who are more responsive to policy [20,21]. One large debate in the literature is which groups of voters are more responsive: a party's core voters or swing voters. Dixit and Londregan [20] generalize two major models [6,22] to highlight the relevant tradeoffs. When parties are homogeneous in their ability to provide benefits to each group of voters, they should target resources to groups with a larger proportion of swing voters. On the other hand, if there are large differences in parties' abilities to provide benefits to a group, perhaps due to providing better suited public goods, parties should target core voters. Our model abstracts from this debate by shutting down both mechanisms that generate targeted transfers. Candidates are symmetric in their ability to provide resources to each group and groups are symmetric in their share of swing voters. Instead, we highlight how asymmetric information can create targeted transfers even in environments with no inherent incentive to target under full information.

The theory of targeting in politics has in part developed by comparing different electoral systems [7,23,24]. Our model shares some features with this literature, particularly in how we model voter preferences. Furthermore, similar to Lindbeck and Weibull [6] and Lizzeri and Persico [7], but differing from Chari et al. [25], we study national candidates who do not represent a single district. Our results on targeting, therefore, are not due to politicians providing benefits to their limited constituency at the expense of the electorate.

A main distinguishing feature between our model and the targeting literature is that we do not assume that all voters are perfectly informed about policy. This feature of our model is closest to a model presented in Mayhew [26] (pp. 52–61). In that model, politicians prefer to provide targeted transfers to their constituents instead of public goods because voters can be certain that the politician deserves credit for the targeted transfers. Our model differs in that voters are not perfectly informed about the politician's platform rather than whether the politician was pivotal in providing the public good. This gives rise to a setting where politicians are more likely to choose targeted policies when they also have a greater ability to target messages and control voter information.

A closely related literature is an intersection of these two strands focusing on the role of media in politics. We share the typical probabilistic voting setup of Strömberg [27], but differ from that paper, Besley and Prat [28], Duggan and Martinelli [29] and Bernhardt et al. [30] by not focusing on the role of (strategic) media actors. While (potentially biased) media surely play an important role in political outcomes [31], we instead study direct communication by candidates for office. Our focus is on the increased ability to target advertisements to voters which is distinguished by its increasing independence from third-party moderation (e.g., via internet advertising).

The two most closely related papers to ours from this literature are Eguia and Nicolò [32] and Gavazza and Lizzeri [33]. In Eguia and Nicolò [32], the authors consider a similar model where each group of voters is potentially uninformed about policies targeting other groups, but are informed about policies targeting their own group. Candidates' platforms may be fully revealed to all voters by some exogenously determined process. The authors then show that equilibria are efficient if voters are sufficiently unlikely to be informed. This stark difference in conclusion is due to two differences in the model. First, candidates may provide public goods to multiple groups of voters in their model. This gives rise to a natural incentive to target under full information, even when universal provision is efficient since candidates can exclude a single group to the benefit of others, giving rise to standard "minimum winning coalition" logic. Second, platforms may be fully revealed exogenously to all voters instead of endogenously partially and asymmetrically revealed. The ability to strategically share partial information with voters is the crucial driver of our results. Gavazza and Lizzeri [33] share the information structure of Eguia and Nicolò [32] but in a model where transfers are always inefficient. We share their conclusion that more information improves efficiency, but differ in our focus on endogenizing the information available to voters.

Finally, Balart et al. [34] study a spatial model of communication technology and advertising expenditure. In their model, candidates first choose platforms. The level of polarization of the platforms determines endogenously the share of informed voters, after which parties choose the level of advertising expenditure. In their model, developments in communication technology are measured by the effectiveness of advertising expenditure. In contrast, our model considers communication technologies in which we explicitly model the increased effectiveness by expanding candidate flexibility over communication. We share similar conclusions in that Balart et al. [34] find that increased effectiveness of advertising drives polarization and increased campaign expenditure, whereas we find that the most flexible communications technologies may lead candidates to select inefficient policy platforms in equilibrium.

3. Model

We build a probabilistic voting model where voters have preferences similar to Lindbeck and Weibull [6] but candidates strategically disclose only a subset of their platform. Differing from other probabilistic voting models, we simplify the setting to one where all voter groups are symmetric with respect to candidates. We make this choice because it removes all incentives for targeting transfers under full information and highlights that our results are due to communication and information asymmetries.

Electoral Competition. There are two candidates (he), a and b, and a measure one of voters (she). Candidates compete in a plurality election by committing to platforms. A platform is an N-dimensional vector that contains *positions* on $N \geq 2$ issues. For each issue $n \in \{1,..,N\}$, a platform contains either the *targeted* position t_n, or the *generic* position g_n. A platform can contain, at most, one targeted position. We refer to the platform that contains only generic positions as the *generic platform* and to the platform that contains targeted position t_n as *targeted platform n*.

Voters are heterogeneous in their preferences and in their ability to observe platforms. Every voter belongs to one of N equally sized (interest) groups. For every issue n, position t_n yields utility $u > 0$

to voters in group n and $-d < 0$ to other voters, while position g_n yields 0 to all voters. We assume $(N-1)d > u$, i.e., the generic platform is the only efficient platform.[6] A fraction $\rho \in (0,1)$ of voters in each group observes the candidates' entire platforms. We refer to these voters as *informed*. The remaining $1-\rho$ voters are *uninformed*. Uninformed voters observe one position from each candidate's platform determined by the message they receive (described below). Uninformed voters in the same group observe the same positions. Voters vote for one of the candidates, and the candidate with the most votes wins the election and implements his platform.

Disclosure. We consider three games corresponding to three different communication technologies. We refer to these games as the *game with random disclosure*, the *game with issue selection* and the *game with microtargeting*. Under random disclosure, after the candidates have selected their platforms, one position at random from each of the two platforms is disclosed to all voters. Each position is equally likely to be disclosed.[7] In the game with issue selection, each candidate selects an issue, and every voter observes the candidate's position on that issue. In the game with microtargeting, each candidate can choose a different position to report to each group of voters.

We make the following restriction on voters' beliefs. Let x and y be two uninformed voters. If in equilibrium candidate i's strategy prescribes the same disclosure for the two voters, then x and y form the same beliefs upon observing the same position of candidate i. Please note that we require x and y to hold the same beliefs both on and off the equilibrium path. This assumption has two implications. First, in the game with random disclosure and the game with issue selection, all uninformed voters, regardless of their group, hold the same beliefs both on and off the equilibrium path. Second, in the game with microtargeting uninformed voters in the same group hold the same beliefs both on and off the equilibrium path.

Timeline. First, candidates simultaneously commit to their platforms. Candidates also choose messages at this stage (under the constraints of the communication technology available to them). Second, uninformed voters receive messages revealing one position from a's platform and one position from b's platform, while informed voters observe both platforms. All voters observe the realization of their idiosyncratic preference shocks (described below) and then cast their votes. The winner of the election is determined, and the winner's platform is implemented.

Payoffs. If candidate $x \in \{a,b\}$ is elected, voter i in group m obtains payoffs $U_{i,m}^x$, where:

$$U_{i,m}^a = \sum_{n=1}^{N} u_m(s_n^a) + \epsilon_i, \quad U_{i,m}^b = \sum_{n=1}^{N} u_m(s_n^b).$$

$s_n^x \in \{g_n, t_n\}$ is the position of candidate x's platform on issue n, while $u_m : \{s_1^x, .., s_N^x\} \to \{-d, 0, u\}$ maps each s_n^x into the corresponding utility for a voter in group m. Voter i's idiosyncratic preference

---

[6] In the next section we discuss the nature of equilibria if $(N-1)d \leq u$.
[7] Please note that we do not assume disclosure to be independent across candidates. Positive correlation between positions disclosed from the two platforms is indeed quite realistic, as a certain issue might raise to prominence in the public discourse during the campaign (we thank an anonymous referee for raising this point).

shock ϵ_i is distributed uniformly on $\left[-\frac{1}{2}, \frac{1}{2}\right]$. We assume that the variance of this shock is large compared to the size of the payoffs that is:[8]

$$\frac{1}{2} > u + (N-1)d.$$

As we assume that voters vote sincerely (see below), an informed voter in group m votes for candidate a with probability

$$\pi^C_{m,a} := \frac{1}{2} + \sum_{n=1}^{N} \left(u_m(s^a_n) - u_m(s^b_n)\right).$$

An uninformed voter in group m, upon observing candidate a's position on issue x (that is, s^a_x) and candidate b's position of issue y (that is, s^b_y) votes for a with probability

$$\pi^P_{m,a} := \frac{1}{2} + \sum_{n=1}^{N} \left(\mathbb{E}_m\left[u_m(s^a_n)|s^a_x\right] - \mathbb{E}_m\left[u_m(s^b_n)|s^b_y\right]\right),$$

where $\mathbb{E}_m$ denotes the voter's expectation conditional on the observed positions. Aggregating over voters, the share of votes for candidate a is (almost surely)

$$\sigma_a := \frac{1}{N} \sum_{m=1}^{N} (\rho \pi^C_{m,a} + (1-\rho) \pi^P_{m,a}),$$

while the share of votes of candidate b is $\sigma_b = 1 - \sigma_a$. Candidates seek to maximize their vote share.

Strategies and equilibrium. The definition of a strategy for the candidates depends on the game considered. In each game, a candidate's strategy selects a platform. In the game with issue selection, each candidate's strategy specifies a single truthful message revealing one position from his platform to all uninformed voters. In the game with microtargeting, each candidate's strategy specifies N truthful messages, each revealing one position from his platform to uninformed voters of one group.

A voter strategy maps her information into a choice of vote. We focus on pure-strategy Nash equilibria in which voters vote for a candidate whose platform they believe will ensure them the highest utility, and off-path beliefs satisfy the restriction mentioned above. We will refer to these as equilibria for convenience. We say that an equilibrium is efficient if the election is won with probability 1 by a candidate that has selected the generic platform, and is inefficient otherwise.

4. Analysis

To establish a benchmark, we first consider the case when all voters are informed.[9] Without uninformed voters, messages are irrelevant and the distinction among the three games is immaterial. Our first proposition states that under perfect observability electoral competition induces candidates to select the generic platform. The proof is in the text.

Proposition 1. *Let $\rho = 1$. In all three games, equilibria exist and are efficient.*

---

[8] This assumption ensures that candidates get a benefit in terms of vote share from their choice of platform proportional to the benefit that voters receive. All our results hold *verbatim* if we assume ϵ_i is distributed uniformly on $\left[-\frac{1}{2\theta}, \frac{1}{2\theta}\right]$ for some θ, as long as $\frac{1}{2\theta} > u + (N-1)d$.

[9] This case is outside the setting described in the previous section, as we assumed $\rho \in (0,1)$.

The proof is immediate. An informed voter in group m votes for candidate a with probability $\pi_{m,a}^C$. Aggregating over voters, candidate a's vote share is

$$\sigma_a = \frac{1}{2} + \frac{1}{N}\sum_{m=1}^{N} \pi_{m,a}^C = \frac{1}{2} + \frac{1}{N}\sum_{m=1}^{N}\sum_{n=1}^{N}\left(u_m(s_n^a) - u_m(s_n^b)\right).$$

For any choice of platform by candidate b, candidate a maximizes σ_a by choosing an efficient platform. Symmetrically, for any choice of platform by candidate a, candidate b maximizes σ_b by choosing an efficient platform. Thus, in equilibrium both candidates commit to the generic platform. The intuition is straightforward: a candidate's vote share is proportional to the utility that his platform ensures to all voters. Thus, an efficient platform maximizes each candidate's vote share.[10]

The same logic applies to an alternative benchmark where candidates cannot send any messages. In a game with no messaging, candidates' platform choices have no effect on their vote share among uninformed voters. Therefore, candidates select platforms to maximize their vote share among informed voters only. The equilibria of such a game are identical to equilibria of a game with perfect observability. Proposition 1 establishes that all equilibria are efficient in this scenario as well. We focus next on settings in which some voters are uninformed, and some informative messages are sent.

4.1. Random Disclosure and Issue Selection

We consider first the games in which microtargeting is not an option. In these games all uninformed voters observe the same position. The next proposition (partially) characterizes the equilibria in these games. The proofs of this and subsequent results are in Appendix A.

Proposition 2. *In the game with random disclosure and in the game with issue selection, equilibria exist and are all efficient.*

In all games we consider, the generic platform ensures more votes from informed voters than a targeted one. The way platforms map into votes from uninformed voters is less straightforward, as these voters only observe one position.

Consider first random disclosure. Suppose a candidate is expected to commit to the generic platform. A deviation to a targeted platform cannot ensure more votes from uninformed voters for the deviating candidate, as all uninformed voters have access to the same information, and there is no platform that is more desirable *on average* for voters than the generic platform. This argument proves existence of an efficient equilibrium. We rule out inefficient equilibria using a similar argument: if a candidate is expected to commit to a targeted platform, a deviation to the generic one never lowers his share of votes from uninformed voters.

Consider now the game with issue selection. In this game candidates have control over messages, but can only select message profiles such that all uninformed voters receive the same message. The arguments used to prove that an efficient equilibrium exists and is unique are similar to the random disclosure case. A targeted platform cannot ensure a candidate's vote share from uninformed voters larger than the generic one, regardless of which position the candidate discloses, as voters, on average, prefer the generic platform, and average preferences determine vote shares

So far we have established that as long as all uninformed voters have access to the same information, electoral competition induces candidates to commit to the efficient platform, regardless of whether candidates control which position is disclosed.

---

10 This is expected as, under perfect observability, our model is a simpler version of Lindbeck and Weibull [6] where voter groups have equal responsiveness to policy.

4.2. Microtargeting

We now relax the constraints on candidates' choice of messages to allow them to send separate messages to each group of voters. The next proposition characterizes equilibria for $N \geq 3$, while $N = 2$ is considered in Proposition 4.

Proposition 3. *Consider the game with microtargeting, and $N \geq 3$. An equilibrium exists. Moreover:*

- *for $\rho < \frac{u-d}{(N-2)d}$ every equilibrium is inefficient;*
- *for $\rho \in \left[\frac{u-d}{(N-2)d}, \frac{u+d}{Nd}\right]$ there exist efficient as well as inefficient equilibria;*
- *for $\rho > \frac{u+d}{Nd}$ every equilibrium is efficient.*

The existence as well as the uniqueness of efficient equilibria for a sufficiently large share of informed voters are, in our view, unsurprising. As ρ gets close to 1 the game resembles the benchmark game with perfect information. As stated in Proposition 1, in this case candidates opt for the generic platform.

We find more striking the existence and the uniqueness of inefficient equilibria for a sufficiently large share of uninformed voters. In these equilibria both candidates commit to a targeted platform.[11] We sketch, in turn, the arguments we use to prove existence and uniqueness of inefficient equilibria.

To prove existence, we construct an equilibrium in which both candidates commit to some targeted platform, and uninformed voters are *skeptical*: they believe a candidate has committed to a targeted platform that ensures them $-d$ unless they observe the position that ensures them u.[12] For these beliefs, a deviation to the generic platform reduces the share of votes from uninformed voters as it results in all uninformed voters incorrectly believing that the candidate has committed to some targeted platform ensuring them $-d$. While this deviation costs the candidate votes from uninformed voters, it increases the candidate's vote share from informed voters. Thus, these inefficient equilibria exist as long as the fraction of informed voters is not too large (we show in the proof that this condition amounts to $\rho \leq \frac{u+d}{Nd}$).

We prove that for $\rho < \frac{u-d}{(N-2)d}$ all equilibria are inefficient using the following argument. In any efficient equilibrium at least one candidate, denote him x, commits to the generic platform and there must be at least one position $s_n^x = g_n$ that is observed by at most one group of voters. Candidate x could deviate to targeted platform n and reveal $s_n^x = t_n$ to uninformed voters in group n, while leaving the choice of issue on which to report his position unchanged for all other groups. Uninformed voters in group n and in at most one other group would be aware of this deviation, while uninformed voters in at least $N-2$ groups would be unaware of it. If $u > d$, this deviation increases candidate x's share of votes from uninformed voters. If moreover ρ is sufficiently small (as we show in the proof, this amounts to $\rho < \frac{u-d}{(N-2)d}$), then the deviation is profitable.

The simplicity of messages relative to platforms is crucial for our results with microtargeting. Intuitively, with richer messages, fewer groups, or simpler platforms, candidates could fully reveal their platform to all groups with their messages. Proposition 4 and Proposition 6, below, explore settings where candidates can fully reveal their platform.

Proposition 3 suggests some interesting comparative statics. Unsurprisingly, a large share of informed voters is associated with efficient equilibria. The relation between equilibrium efficiency and the benefit to receiving a targeted policy, u, is instead non-monotonic. For large u ($u \geq d(N-1)$)

---

[11] A hypothetical equilibrium in which a candidate commits to a targeted platform and the other commits to the generic one would be efficient, as the candidate committing to the generic platform would always win the election, due to voters holding correct beliefs on path.
[12] Please note that skeptical beliefs require voters from different groups to interpret the same out-of equilibrium position in different ways. This does not contradict our equilibrium restriction on beliefs, as on path these voters observe different positions.

targeted platforms are efficient, and so are all equilibria: while we have not considered this parametric region in our analysis, proving that for parameters in this region in equilibrium both candidates choose a targeted platform is straightforward. For smaller u ($u < d(N-1)$), efficient equilibria exist and inefficient equilibria can be ruled out only if u is sufficiently small relative to ρ to dissuade candidates from committing to inefficient targeted platforms.[13] In the limit, as u approaches 0, efficient equilibria always exist, and if additionally $\rho > \frac{1}{N}$, only efficient equilibria exist. A symmetric exercise can be done for d.

Finally, we show that as positions become more narrowly targeted, inefficient equilibria become easier to sustain. Specifically, we consider what happens as N gets larger, yet u also changes, so that $\frac{u-(N-1)d}{N}$ does not change. In this case, the social welfare associated with a targeted policy stays constant, while the benefits accrue to a smaller group. Let $K = \frac{u-(N-1)d}{N}$. We can write the two thresholds from Proposition 3 as $\frac{u-d}{(N-2)d} = 1 + \frac{KN}{(N-2)d}$ and $\frac{u+d}{Nd} = 1 + \frac{K}{d}$. The first threshold becomes larger as N increases. As the benefit becomes more narrowly targeted, $\frac{(N-1)d}{N}$ increases. Thus, $\frac{u}{N}$ must also increase for $K = \frac{u}{N} - \frac{(N-1)d}{N}$ to hold. As a result, inefficient equilibria become easier to sustain, as deviations from a targeted platform to the generic one result in a loss of votes from uninformed voters proportional to $\frac{u}{N}$. The second threshold is constant with respect to N for constant K. To complete the comparative statics over N, the next proposition characterizes the equilibria for $N = 2$.

Proposition 4. *In the game with microtargeting and $N = 2$, equilibria exist and are all efficient.*

When only two targeted platforms are available, a candidate that commits to the generic platform can credibly show to any uninformed voter that he did not commit to the platform ensuring her $-d$. Doing so simply requires candidate x to send message $s_1^x = g_1$ to voters in group 2 and $s_2^x = g_2$ to voters in group 1. In this context, the generic platform is a candidate's optimal choice.

5. Extensions

The core components of our model can be generalized in many directions. One could, for example, consider what would happen if informed voters only observed subsets of platforms. This is perhaps a more natural assumption; even if candidates have well-defined positions on all possible issues during the campaign, they rarely disclose all of them publicly. In this case, even informed voters may lack information on some components of candidate platforms. It is easy to verify that our games with a fraction ρ of informed voters are for all practical purposes identical to games in which every informed voter observes m issues, selected at random, from each platform and the fraction of informed voters is $\frac{\rho N}{m}$. It should also be straightforward to extend our analysis to allow for heterogeneity in the size of the groups, variance of the idiosyncratic shock across groups, or in the payoffs associated with targeted platforms.[14]

We present here two extensions that shed further light on the inefficiencies in the game with microtargeting. First, we consider elections in which candidates can only choose policies to target a subset of groups. Second, we allow candidates to use "negative advertising". We model negative advertising as candidates having the ability to send messages disclosing a position from their opponent's platform.

---

[13] At the same time, as u increases the loss of social welfare associated with inefficient platforms changes in a non-monotonic, convex way.
[14] The first two of these features are common for probabilistic voting models and generate targeted transfers. We suppress them in our main analysis to shut off an alternate rationale for targeting.

5.1. Limited Policy Targeting

This subsection generalizes the game with microtargeting by assuming that candidates can select a targeted position only on one of the first $M \leq N$ issues.[15] We call this the game with limited policy targeting. The next two propositions characterize the equilibria of this game. They show that the size of M affects the prevalence, but not the existence, of inefficient equilibria. As the number of available targeted platforms decreases, it becomes easier to sustain equilibria in which candidates commit to the generic platform. As long as candidates can choose among different targeted platforms, however, the existence of inefficient equilibria is not affected by the size of M.

Proposition 5. *Consider the game with limited policy targeting. Let $M > 1$, $N > 2$, and define $\bar{n} := \max\{n \in \{1, .., N\} | n \leq \frac{N}{M}\}$. Equilibria exist, and in equilibrium:*

- *if $\rho < \frac{u - \bar{n}d}{d(N - (1 + \bar{n}))}$ every equilibrium is inefficient;*
- *if $\rho \in \left[\frac{u - \bar{n}d}{d(N - (1 + \bar{n}))}, \frac{u + d}{Nd}\right]$ both efficient and inefficient equilibria exist;*
- *if $\rho > \frac{u + d}{Nd}$ every equilibrium is efficient.*

As long as $M > 1$, inefficient equilibria exist. To prove the existence of inefficient equilibria we construct, once more, equilibria in which uninformed voters hold skeptical beliefs. In these equilibria, candidates do not find it profitable to commit to the generic platform because uninformed voters interpret a disclosure of a generic position as a signal that the candidate committed to a targeted platform that yields them $-d$. Inefficient equilibria require at least 2 possible targeted platforms; otherwise, a candidate could fully reveal his commitment to the generic platform to all voters.

Nevertheless, as M decreases, efficient equilibria exist for a larger interval of values of ρ.[16] To minimize the incentive for a candidate to deviate from the generic platform, every uninformed voter should expect to observe $s_n^x = g_n$ for some $n \in \{1, .., M\}$. As M decreases, the share of uninformed voters expecting to observe $s_n^x = g_n$ can get larger for all $n \in \{1, .., M\}$. As a result, more uninformed voters are aware of any eventual deviation to a targeted platform, thus making such deviation less profitable for a candidate.

In the extreme case where $M = 1$, all uninformed voters would observe a deviation from equilibrium. Thus, efficient equilibria exist for any fraction of informed voters. Intuitively, this is because each candidate can credibly commit to each voter to not target any other voter. Proposition 6 also records that all equilibria are efficient if $M = 1$. This is also intuitive, as candidates can credibly communicate to all voters their choice of platform, corresponding to the result in Proposition 1.[17]

Proposition 6. *Consider the game with M targeted platforms. Let $M = 1$. Equilibria exists and are efficient.*

5.2. Negative Advertising

This subsection generalizes the game with microtargeting by allowing candidates to disclose a position from either platform. The game with negative advertising differs from the game with microtargeting only in one aspect: candidates observe their opponent's platform and, for each group of voters, they can opt to disclose a position from their own platform, or from the other candidate's platform. Proposition 7 records that in this case, efficient equilibria exist for all parameter values, while inefficient equilibria exist for the same parameter values as in the game with microtargeting.

---

[15] The game with random disclosure and the game with issue selection could be generalized in the same way. Equilibria in those games are efficient regardless of the size of M.
[16] To verify this, observe that larger M yield smaller $\bar{n}$, and $\frac{u - \bar{n}d}{d(N - (1 + \bar{n}))}$ is decreasing in $\bar{n}$.
[17] The proof of Proposition 6 is available upon request.

Proposition 7. *In the game with negative advertising, efficient equilibria exist. Moreover, if $N > 2$ and $\rho \leq \frac{u+d}{Nd}$, there exist also inefficient equilibria.*

The possibility to disclose a position from the opponent's platform ensures that efficient equilibria exist. In these equilibria candidates commit to the generic platform as they anticipate that if they were to deviate to a targeted platform, the opponent would disclose their targeted position. The possibility to disclose a position from the opponent's platform does not, however, rule out inefficient equilibria. To show existence of inefficient equilibria we rely, once again, on skeptical beliefs of uninformed voters. We let candidates commit to a targeted platform and uninformed voters believe that a candidate has chosen a platform yielding $-d$ unless they are shown evidence that he chose the platform that yields them u. If the share of informed voters is sufficiently small, a deviation to the generic platform is not profitable.

6. Conclusions

We have shown how policy targeting, when coupled with message targeting, can lead to inefficiencies in candidates' choice of platforms. While models of policy targeting abound in the literature on electoral competition, these models usually do not distinguish between policy and communication. We view this paper as a first step in a larger research program that differentiates between these types of targeting and studies their interaction.

Our model relies on some voters being largely uninformed about policy platforms. These uninformed voters base their decisions on simple, but truthful, messages from candidates revealing a subset of policy platforms. Our model recovers the standard efficient allocation when policy is perfectly observable by all voters. When candidates can reveal different components of their platform to different groups of voters, candidates trade off the gain in votes from targeting a subset of uninformed voters at the cost of losing some votes from informed voters. When the share of informed voters is sufficiently small, equilibria under microtargeting are inefficient.

In this paper, we present a very simple model which distinguishes between targeted policies and targeted communication. Much of the literature on policy targeting has instead explored how the incentives to target differ by electoral system. Such an extension of our model would also be interesting. Similarly, considering a richer menu of policies or exploring competition with more than two candidates could generate more nuanced predictions. As more data about voters become available, politicians can learn more about and better differentiate between narrow groups of voters. It would be interesting to explore the effects of this knowledge coupled with a superior ability to target messages. More broadly, the increased availability of voters' data and simultaneous advances in marketing techniques have made targeted political communication a timely and policy relevant area of research: Andrew Yang has made individual property rights over personalized data a central plank of his 2020 US presidential primary platform.

Finally, testing our model empirically would be interesting but also poses some challenges. The share of informed voters, returns to targeted policies, and costs of financing targeted policies are essential to the predictions of our model, but difficult to measure in practice. Given such measures, an ideal empirical setting would consider multiple constituencies with exogenous variation in the ability of candidates to target ads. One possible way would be to exploit variation in internet penetration across districts as targeting online advertising is substantially more flexible than alternative forms of media. An alternative test could exploit the share of informed voters, holding constant the ability to target. Such a test could exploit variation in self-sought information on platforms (e.g., measured via online search frequency across districts) as a proxy for informed voters since such information cannot be targeted as precisely. Both methods, however, rely on satisfactory proxies for the previously mentioned unobserved parameters.

Author Contributions: Conceptualization, J.B. and B.S.; methodology, J.B. and B.S.; validation, J.B. and B.S.; formal analysis, J.B.; writing—original draft preparation, J.B. and B.S.; writing—review and editing, J.B. and B.S.

Funding: This research received no external funding.

Acknowledgments: We thank the Editor, Gabriele Gratton, and two anonymous referees for helpful remarks and suggestions. We also thank Laurent Bouton, Fenella Carpena, Mads Greaker, Tapas Kundu, Antoine Loeper, Juan Margitic, Gisle Natvik, Allison Stashko, and Nicholas Yannelis for helpful comments and discussions.

Conflicts of Interest: The authors declare no conflict of interest.

Appendix A. Proofs of Propositions

Proof of Proposition 2. An efficient platform ensures more votes from informed voters than an inefficient one in all the games we consider (see Proposition 1). Call this Observation 1.

Consider first the game with random disclosure. Let $\mathbb{E}[\pi_{m,a}^{P*}]$ denote candidate a's expected vote share from uninformed voters in group m in equilibrium. Let instead $\mathbb{E}[\pi_{m,a}^{P\dagger}]$ denote a's expected vote share from uninformed voters in group m if a deviates to an out-of-equilibrium platform while b does not. Then a's expected gain (or loss) of votes from uninformed voters as a result of the deviation is

$$\sum_{m=1}^{N} \mathbb{E}[\pi_{m,a}^{P*}] - \sum_{m=1}^{N} \mathbb{E}[\pi_{m,a}^{P\dagger}] =$$

$$\sum_{m=1}^{N} (\mathbb{E}[\pi_{m,a}^{P*}] - \mathbb{E}[\pi_{m,a}^{P\dagger}]) =$$

$$\sum_{m=1}^{N} \sum_{n=1}^{N} \left(\frac{\mathbb{E}_m[\sum_{i=1}^{N} u_m(s_i^a)|s_n^{a*}]) - \mathbb{E}_m[\sum_{i=1}^{N} u_m(s_i^a)|s_n^{a\dagger}]}{N} \right),$$

where s_n^{a*} and $s_n^{a\dagger}$ denote the positions of candidate a on issue n, in equilibrium and following the deviation, respectively. Clearly this difference is independent of the platform choice of b, and independent of the correlation between disclosures from the two candidate's platform. We will repeatedly take advantage of this observation in our proof.

We first show that there exists an equilibrium in which both candidates commit to the generic platform (this equilibrium is efficient). A deviation in this equilibrium amounts to committing to a targeted platform. Suppose candidate a deviates to targeted platform 1. If uninformed voters observe $s_n^a = g_n$ for $n \neq 1$, the deviation leaves the share of votes from uninformed voters for candidate a unchanged. If instead they observe $s_1^a = t_1$, the share of votes for candidate a from uninformed voters changes by $(1-\rho)\frac{u-(N-1)d}{N} < 0$ as a result of the deviation. Hence $\sum_{m=1}^{N} \mathbb{E}[\pi_{m,a}^{P*}] - \sum_{m=1}^{N} \mathbb{E}[\pi_{m,a}^{P\dagger}] = (1-\rho)\frac{u-(N-1)d}{N^2} < 0$. Observation 1 implies that the deviation is not profitable. By symmetry of targeted platforms and candidates, candidates have no profitable deviation, thus we have indeed constructed an equilibrium.

To show that all equilibria are efficient, we prove by contradiction that in equilibrium both candidates commit to the generic platform. Suppose in equilibrium candidate a commits to targeted platform 1. Consider a deviation to the generic platform. The share of uninformed-voter votes for candidate a changes only if $s_1^a = g_1$ is disclosed. In this case, either all uninformed voters believe that candidate a has committed to some targeted platform $n \neq 1$, then candidate a's share of votes from uninformed voters does not change as a result of the deviation, or else they all believe that he has committed to the generic platform, hence his share of votes from uninformed voters changes by $(1-\rho)\frac{(N-1)d-u}{N} > 0$. As the deviation increases the share of votes from informed voters (Observation 1), the deviation is profitable, yielding a contradiction.

Consider now the game with issue selection. We first show that there exists an efficient equilibrium in which candidates commit to the generic platform. To check that there does not exist a profitable deviation, note that in equilibrium all uninformed voters hold the same beliefs both on and off path, hence any deviation that changes uninformed voters' beliefs cannot increase the share of votes from uninformed voters. Thus, by Observation 1, there is no profitable deviation.

Next, we establish that all equilibria are efficient. Suppose in equilibrium candidate x commits to targeted platform n. Consider a deviation that requires to commit to the generic platform. This deviation increases the share of votes from informed voters. Regardless of the choice of disclosure in equilibrium and the choice of disclosure associated with the deviation, the share of votes from uninformed voters cannot get smaller as a result of the deviation, as all uninformed voters hold the same beliefs both on and off path. The deviation is thus profitable. □

Proof of Proposition 3. We say that an uninformed voter holds *skeptical beliefs* if, upon observing an out-of-equilibrium position $s_n^x = g_n$, she believes that candidate x's platform yields her utility $-d$.

In the first half of the proof we show that inefficient equilibria exists if and only if $\rho \leq \frac{u+d}{Nd}$. We begin by showing that an inefficient equilibrium exists if $\rho \leq \frac{u+d}{Nd}$. Consider a tentative equilibrium in which both candidates commit to targeted platform 1 and disclose, respectively, positions s_n^a and s_n^b to uninformed voters in group n, while uninformed voters hold skeptical beliefs. It is easy to check that a deviation that requires to commit to targeted platform 1 while changing the choice of disclosure, or to commit to a different targeted platform together with some choice of disclosure, cannot be profitable. Consider a deviation that requires to commit to the generic platform. The deviation ensures $\rho \frac{(N-1)d-u}{N}$ extra votes from informed voters. At the same time, as a result of the deviation, for any choice of disclosure all uninformed voters believe that the candidate's platform yields them $-d$; hence the deviation results in a loss of $(1-\rho)\frac{u+d}{N}$ votes from uninformed voters. As long as $\rho \leq \frac{u+d}{Nd}$ this deviation is not profitable, and therefore there is no profitable deviation, and our tentative equilibrium is indeed an equilibrium.

Next we show that inefficient equilibria exist only if $\rho \leq \frac{u+d}{Nd}$. We do so by showing that in equilibrium both candidates commit to the generic platform if $\rho > \frac{u+d}{Nd}$. Suppose in equilibrium candidate x commits to targeted platform n. Consider a deviation that requires to commit to the generic platform while leaving unchanged the choice of issues to report on. The deviation cannot decrease the share of votes from uninformed voters that do not belong to group n, regardless of the issue on which they observe candidate x's position. Thus, as a result of the deviation candidate x loses, at most, $(1-\rho)\frac{u+d}{N}$ votes from uninformed voters. As the deviation yields $\rho\frac{(N-1)d-u}{N}$ additional votes from informed voters, the deviation is profitable if $\rho > \frac{u+d}{Nd}$.

In the second half of the proof we establish that efficient equilibria exist if and only if $\rho \geq \frac{u-d}{d(N-2)}$.

We begin by showing that if $\rho \geq \frac{u-d}{d(N-2)}$ then there exists an equilibrium in which both candidates commit to the generic platform and report to group 1 about (their position on) issue 2, to group 2 about issue 3 and so on, and to group N about issue 1, while uninformed voters hold skeptical beliefs. Deviating to a different disclosure while committing to the generic platform is not profitable. Consider a deviation that requires to commit to targeted platform 1, while disclosing $s_1^x = t_1$ to uninformed voters in groups 1 and N, and disclosing as required by the equilibrium strategy to all other uninformed voters. The deviation is not profitable as long as: $\rho\frac{u-(N-1)d}{N} + (1-\rho)\frac{u-d}{N} \leq 0$, or equivalently: $\rho \geq \frac{u-d}{d(N-2)}$. Whenever this deviation is not profitable, there is no profitable deviation.

We conclude by showing that all equilibria are inefficient if $\rho < \frac{u-d}{d(N-2)}$. Suppose in equilibrium candidate x is expected to commit to the generic platform. Please note that there must be at least one position that is reported to no more than one group of voters. Let g_n be such a position. Consider a deviation that requires to commit to targeted platform n, while disclosing $s_n^x = t_n$ to group n and any group that in equilibrium observes $s_n^x = g_n$, while leaving the disclosure unchanged for all other groups. The deviation is profitable as long as $\rho\frac{u-(N-1)d}{N} + (1-\rho)\frac{u-d}{N} > 0$, or equivalently $\rho < \frac{u-d}{d(N-2)}$. This concludes the proof. □

Proof of Proposition 4. We first show that an efficient equilibrium exists. Consider a strategy that requires candidate x to commit to the generic platform while disclosing $s_1^x = g_1$ to uninformed voters in group 2 and $s_2^x = g_2$ to uninformed voters in group 1. Consider a candidate equilibrium in which both candidates adopt the strategy just defined and uninformed voters hold skeptical beliefs (see the proof of Proposition 3 for a definition of skeptical beliefs). To verify that candidates do not have a profitable deviation, note first that a deviation that requires to commit to the generic platform and adopt a different disclosure results in a smaller share of votes from uninformed voters and does not change the share of votes from informed voters. At the same time, a deviation that requires to commit to a targeted platform cannot be profitable, as it results in a change in the share of votes from uninformed voters not larger than $\frac{(1-\rho)u-d}{2} < 0$, and in a reduction in the share of votes from informed voters.

Next, we show that all equilibria are efficient. Suppose that in equilibrium candidate x is expected to commit to a targeted platform. Consider a deviation that requires to commit to the generic platform while disclosing $s_1^x = g_1$ to uninformed voters in group 2 and $s_2^x = g_2$ to uninformed voters in group 1. This deviation results in a larger share of votes from informed voters, and also ensures that every uninformed voter expects a utility at least as large as 0 from candidate x's platform. As targeted platforms ensure less than 0 to the average voter, candidate x's share of votes from uninformed voters increases as a result of the deviation. □

Proof of Proposition 5. The proof that inefficient equilibria exist if and only if $\rho \leq \frac{u+d}{Nd}$ is the same as in the proof of Proposition 3.

We establish here that efficient equilibria exist if and only if $\rho \geq \frac{u-\bar{n}d}{d(N-(1+\bar{n}))}$. We first establish that there exists an equilibrium in which both candidates commit to the generic platform and disclose in a way that ensures that for each $n \in \{1,..,M\}$: $s_n^a = g_n$ (respectively, $s_n^b = g_n$) is disclosed to at least $\bar{n}$ different groups, and voters in group n do not observe $s_n^a = g_n$ (respectively, $s_n^b = g_n$). Suppose moreover that voters hold skeptical beliefs (as defined in the proof of Proposition 3). Deviating to a different disclosure while committing to the generic platform is not profitable. Please note that for any candidate x there is at least one issue $n \in \{1,..,M\}$ such that candidate x discloses s_n^x to $\bar{n}$ groups. Let issue 1 be such an issue. Consider a deviation that requires to commit to targeted platform 1, while disclosing $s_1^x = t_1$ to group 1 and disclosing positions from the same issues as prescribed by the equilibrium strategy to all others. The deviation is not profitable as long as: $\rho \frac{u-(N-1)d}{N} + (1-\rho)\frac{u-\bar{n}d}{N} \leq 0$, or equivalently: $\rho \geq \frac{u-\bar{n}d}{d(N-(1+\bar{n}))}$. It is immediate that whenever this deviation is not profitable, then all deviations are not profitable.

Next, we show that all equilibria are inefficient if $\rho < \frac{u-\bar{n}d}{d(N-(1+\bar{n}))}$. Suppose in equilibrium candidate x commits to the generic platform. Please note that there must be at least one issue $n \in \{1,..,M\}$ such that voters in no more than $\bar{n}$ groups observe $s_n^a = g_n$. Let issue 1 be such an issue. A deviation to targeted platform 1 is profitable as long as $\rho \frac{u-(N-1)d}{N} + (1-\rho)\frac{u-\bar{n}d}{N} > 0$, or equivalently: $\rho < \frac{u-\bar{n}d}{d(N-(1+\bar{n}))}$. □

Proof of Proposition 7. We first show that an efficient equilibrium exists. Consider the following strategies. Both candidates commit to the generic platform and, as long as they do not observe a deviation by the other candidate, they disclose their own position on issue 1 to all uninformed voters. If candidate x deviates to targeted platform n, the other candidate reports $s_n^x = t_n$ to all uninformed voters. Uninformed voters believe that a candidate has committed to the generic platform, unless they observe a targeted position from his platform. It is easy to check that there is no profitable deviation for the candidates.

Next, we show that inefficient equilibria exist if $\rho \leq \frac{u+d}{Nd}$. Consider the following strategies: both candidates commit to targeted platform 1, and disclose their own position on issue n to uninformed voters in group n, regardless of the choice of platform of the other candidate. Uninformed voters believe that a candidate has committed a platform that ensures them $-d$ unless either they observe that the candidate has committed to the platform that ensures them u, or, for $N = 3$, they observe two positions showing that the candidate has not committed to either of the two platforms that ensure them $-d$. A deviation to commit to a different targeted platform cannot be profitable regardless of the choice of disclosure. A deviation to the generic platform results in the same payoff regardless of what position is disclosed. Such a deviation is profitable if and only if $\rho \frac{((N-1)d-u)}{N} \geq (1-\rho)\frac{u+d}{N}$, which is equivalent to $\rho \geq \frac{u+d}{Nd}$. □

References

1. Gentzkow, M.; Shapiro, J.M. Ideological Segregation Online and Offline. *Q. J. Econ.* **2011**, *126*, 1799–1839. [CrossRef]
2. Ridout, T.; Franz, M.; Goldstein, K.; Feltus, W. Separation by Television Program: Understanding the Targeting of Political Advertising in Presidential Elections. *Political Commun.* **2012**, *29*, 1–23. [CrossRef]
3. Bennet, C. Voter databases, micro-targeting, and data protection law: can political parties campaign in Europe as they do in North America? *Int. Data Priv. Law* **2016**, *6*, 261–275. [CrossRef]
4. Anstead, N. Data-Driven Campaigning in the 2015 United Kingdom General Election. *Int. J. Press.* **2017**, *22*, 294–313. [CrossRef]
5. Goldfarb, A.; Tucker, C. Digital Economics. *J. Econ. Lit.* **2019**, *57*, 3–43. [CrossRef]
6. Lindbeck, A.; Weibull, J.W. Balanced-budget redistribution as the outcome of political competition. *Public Choice* **1987**, *52*, 273–297. [CrossRef]
7. Lizzeri, A.; Persico, N. The Provision of Public Goods under Alternative Electoral Incentives. *Am. Econ. Rev.* **2001**, *91*, 225–239. [CrossRef]
8. Coibion, O.; Gorodnichenko, Y. Is the Phillips Curve Alive and Well After All? Inflation Expectations and the Missing Disinflation. *Am. Econ. J. Macroecon.* **2015**, *7*, 197–232. [CrossRef]
9. DellaVigna, S.; Pollet, J.M. Investor Inattention and Friday Earnings Announcements. *J. Financ.* **2009**, *64*, 709–749. [CrossRef]
10. Carpini, M.X.D.; Keeter, S. *What Americans Know about Politics and Why It Matters*; Yale University Press: New Haven, CT, USA, 1996.
11. Tyson, S.A. Information Acquisition, Strategic Voting, and Improving the Quality of Democratic Choice. *J. Politics* **2016**, *78*, 1016–1031. doi:10.1086/686027. [CrossRef]
12. Elmendorf, C.; Wood, A. Elite Political Ignorance: Law, Data, and the Representation of (Mis)Perceived Electorates. *Davis Law Rev.* **2018**, *53*, 571–636. [CrossRef]
13. Zuiderveen Borgesius, F.; Moller, J.; Kruikemeier, S.; Ó Fathaigh, R.; Irion, K.; Dobber, T.; Bodo, B.; de Vreese, C. Online Political Microtargeting: Promises and Threats for Democracy. *Utrecht Law Rev.* **2017**, *14*, 82–96. [CrossRef]
14. Bagwell, K. *The Economics of Advertising*; Edward Elgar Publishing: Cheltenham, UK, 2001.
15. Schipper, B.; Woo, H.Y. Political Awareness, Microtargeting of Voters, and Negative Electoral Campaigning. *Q. J. Political Sci.* **2019**, *14*, 41–88. [CrossRef]
16. Gratton, G.; Holden, R.; Kolotilin, A. When to Drop a Bombshell. *Rev. Econ. Stud.* **2017**, *85*, 2139–2172. [CrossRef]
17. Ogden, B. The Imperfect Beliefs Voting Model. 2016. Available online: https://ssrn.com/abstract=2431447 (accessed on 28 June 2019).
18. Aragonès, E.; Castanheira, M.; Giani, M. Electoral Competition through Issue Selection. *Am. J. Political Sci.* **2015**, *59*, 71–90. [CrossRef]
19. Demange, G.; Van der Straeten, K. Communicating on electoral platforms. *J. Econ. Behav. Org.* **2017**. [CrossRef]
20. Dixit, A.; Londregan, J. Redistributive Politics and Economic Efficiency. *Am. Political Sci. Rev.* **1995**, *89*, 856–866. [CrossRef]
21. Dixit, A.; Londregan, J. The Determinants of Success of Special Interests in Redistributive Politics. *J. Politics* **1996**, *58*, 1132–1155. [CrossRef]
22. Cox, G.W.; McCubbins, M.D. Electoral Politics as a Redistributive Game. *J. Politics* **1986**, *48*, 370–389. [CrossRef]
23. Lizzeri, A.; Persico, N. A drawback of Electoral Competition. *J. Eur. Econ. Assoc.* **2005**, *3*, 1318–1348. [CrossRef]
24. Genicot, G.; Bouton, L.; Castanheira, M. *Electoral Systems and Inequalities in Government Interventions*. Technical Report; National Bureau of Economic Research: Cambridge, MA, USA, 2018.

25. Chari, V.V.; Jones, L.E.; Marimon, R. The Economics of Split-Ticket Voting in Representative Democracies. *Am. Econ. Rev.* **1997**, *87*, 957–976.
26. Mayhew, D.R. *Congress: The Electoral Connection*; Yale University Press: New Haven, CT, USA, 1974; Volume 26.
27. Strömberg, D. Mass Media Competition, Political Competition, and Public Policy. *Rev. Econ. Stud.* **2004**, *71*, 265–284. [CrossRef]
28. Besley, T.; Prat, A. Handcuffs for the Grabbing Hand? Media Capture and Government Accountability. *Am. Econ. Rev.* **2006**, *96*, 720–736. [CrossRef]
29. Duggan, J.; Martinelli, C. A Spatial Theory of Media Slant and Voter Choice. *Rev. Econ. Stud.* **2011**, *78*, 640–666. [CrossRef]
30. Bernhardt, D.; Krasa, S.; Polborn, M. Political polarization and the electoral effects of media bias. *J. Public Econ.* **2008**, *92*, 1092–1104. [CrossRef]
31. DellaVigna, S.; Kaplan, E. The Fox News Effect: Media Bias and Voting. *Q. J. Econ.* **2007**, *122*, 1187–1234. [CrossRef]
32. Eguia, J.X.; Nicolò, A. Information and targeted spending. *Theor. Econ.* **2019**, *14*, 373–402. [CrossRef]
33. Gavazza, A.; Lizzeri, A. Transparency and Economic Policy. *Rev. Econ. Stud.* **2009**, *76*, 1023–1048. [CrossRef]
34. Balart, P.; Casas, A.; Troumpounis, O. Technological Changes, Campaign Spending, And Polarization. Working Paper. 2018. Available online: https://editorialexpress.com/cgi-bin/conference/download.cgi?db_name=EWM2018&paper_id=276 (accessed on 28 June 2019).

© 2019 by the authors. Licensee MDPI, Basel, Switzerland. This article is an open access article distributed under the terms and conditions of the Creative Commons Attribution (CC BY) license (http://creativecommons.org/licenses/by/4.0/).

Article
A Note on Pivotality

Addison Pan

Department of Economics, University of Auckland Business School, Sir Owen G Glenn Building, 12 Grafton Rd, Auckland 1010, New Zealand; addison.pan@auckland.ac.nz; Tel.: +64-9-923-2406

Received: 4 April 2019; Accepted: 29 May 2019; Published: 1 June 2019

Abstract: This note provides simple derivations of the equilibrium conditions for different voting games with incomplete information. In the standard voting game à la Austen-Smith and Banks (1996), voters update their beliefs, and, conditional on their being pivotal, cast their votes. However, in voting games such as those of Ellis (2016) and Fabrizi, Lippert, Pan, and Ryan (2019), given a closed and convex set of priors, ambiguity-averse voters would select a prior from this set in a strategy-contingent manner. As a consequence, both the pivotal and non-pivotal events matter to voters when deciding their votes. In this note, I demonstrate that for ambiguous voting games the conditional probability of being pivotal alone is no longer sufficient to determine voters' best responses.

Keywords: jury trial; pivotality; ambiguity

JEL Classification: D71; D72; D81

1. Introduction

Since Austen-Smith and Banks [1] pointed out that sincere voting may not constitute a Nash Equilibrium of a voting game with incomplete information, a series of papers and startling results based on their basic model have followed. This is so, in spite of the many criticisms surrounding the assumptions of their model provided, for instance, by Margolis [2–4] and Dietrich and Spiekermann [5,6]. The main critique of these authors is the blunt application of game theory to political science: Since these results rely on the pivotality condition, the results so obtained are, simply put, unrealistic and too surprising to be useful to predict real-world behaviour. The idea that voters determine their votes only by conditioning on them being pivotal, i.e., in the event that they affect the voting outcome, is considered to be too reductive of what drives voting behaviour.

However, this is not as heroic as it is accused of being as an equilibrium condition in a normative sense when strategic voting akin to that defined by Austen-Smith and Banks [1] is considered. It remains to be proved whether pivotality is a necessary and sufficient condition for Bayesian Nash Equilibria of other strategic voting games. That is, whether, in the presence of ambiguity, the equilibrium also depends on the evaluation of events in which the voter is not pivotal.

In essence, the establishment of the pivotal logic is a result of the expected utility assumption in instrumental voting models, inter alia, those of Austen-Smith and Banks [1] and Feddersen and Pesendorfer [7]. In these models, instrumental voters determine their votes, conditional on the probability that their votes affect the final outcome of the voting game. Voters compute the expected payoffs of different actions and define their best responses.

In the model of Austen-Smith and Banks [1], the instrumental voters have a single common prior. Hence, the probability of each non-pivotal event is a singleton and is act-independent. As a consequence of the expected utility assumption, when a voter is confronted with such events, not only their vote does not affect the voting outcome, but also the expected utility under non-pivotality cancels out. As a consequence, the only remaining component that matters is when the voter is pivotal.

This implies that the pivotality condition is a necessary and sufficient condition for the Bayesian Nash voting equilibria to be established.

Conversely, in voting games with subjective uncertainty, such as those of Ellis [8] and Fabrizi et al. [9], given a closed and convex set of priors, ambiguity-averse voters would select a prior from this set in a strategy-contingent manner. As a result, although voters' strategies do not change their pay-offs in non-pivotal states, they affect their subjective beliefs with respect to the relevant states. Hence, the expected utility under non-pivotality need not cancel out. Instead, voters update their beliefs, and conditionally both on their being pivotal and non-pivotal, cast their votes. In the model of Ellis [8], voters have the Maxmin preferences as in [10]. Thus, they prefer randomising to hedge the subjective uncertainty. This results in the failure of information aggregation in collective voting under ambiguity.

In this note, I provide a more explicit proof for the equilibrium condition for a general common-value voting model under ambiguity. I give a more detailed proof than Austen-Smith and Banks [1] did in their appendix. With an extended set of notations, I define general voting games under ambiguity. I check the equilibrium conditions for voting games with ambiguity such as those in Ellis [8]. Additionally, I generalise the results of Ellis [8] to the case with ambiguity about the conditional distribution of signals and illustrate the equilibrium conditions for voting games such as Fabrizi et al.'s [9].

In contrast to Austen-Smith and Banks [1], in the latter models, I show that the pivotality condition alone is not sufficient to determine voters' best responses. Hence, even in an instrumental voting setup, the relaxation of the expected utility assumption—for instance, when voters are Maxmin expected utility maximisers under a close and convex set of priors—makes a prominent difference in terms of how voters determine their voting behaviours.

Besides Ellis [8] and Fabrizi et al. [9], there are several other authors discussing the modification of the pivotal logic beyond the expected utility, even when maintaining the pivotal voter assumption. Respectively, Eliaz, Ray, and Razin [11] and Dillenberger and Raymond [12] relaxed the expected utility assumption by allowing voters to have rank-dependent preferences (as in Quiggin [13]) and quasi-convex preferences. These two studies not only provide explanations for the choice shifts observed in the group voting context but also reveal that voters may base their decisions on non-pivotal events.

This note proceeds as follows. In Section 2, I carefully derive pivotality conditions for voting games as those considered by Austen-Smith and Banks [1]. In Section 3, I define the ambiguous voting game and show the equilibrium condition for it. I also use the models of Ellis [8] and Fabrizi et al. [9] to illustrate the insufficiency of conditioning merely on pivotality. The last section concludes.

2. Pivotality in Austen-Smith and Banks [1]

I present the voting model of Austen-Smith and Banks [1] as a game with incomplete information in the following way: There is a set of $I = \{1, 2, \cdots, n\}$ voters, who have to vote over two alternatives; assume that n is odd and $n \geq 3$. Denote by $\Theta = \{A, B\}$ the set of states of nature. Each voter has an action set $V_i = \{A, B\}$, in which A means "choose alternative A" and B means "choose alternative B". Before voters simultaneously cast their votes, each receives an independent private signal $t_i \in T_i = \{a, b\}$. Thus, T_i is the type set of voter i. The signals are assumed to be conditionally independent given the state of nature. Let $\Omega = \Theta \times T$ be the set of the states of the world, where $T = \times_{i \in I} T_i$. Then, let the probability $\pi \in \Delta(\Omega)$ be the common prior, which is the joint probability distribution of the state of nature and types of all voters, such that,

$$\pi(A) = p, \quad \pi(B) = 1 - p;$$

and

$$\pi(t, \theta) = \pi(\theta)\pi(t|\theta) = \pi(\theta) \times_{i \in I} r_\theta(t_i),$$

where $t = (t_1, \ldots, t_n) \in T$ is the type profile and $r_\theta \in \Delta(T_i)$ is the probability of receiving the signal a or b conditional on $\theta \in \Theta$. Therefore, a type profile t is drawn according to the prior $\pi(t)$ over T, that is,

$$\pi(t) = p r_A(t) + (1-p) r_B(t),$$

where $r_A(a) \in (1/2, 1)$ and $r_B(b) \in (1/2, 1)$.

Given $k \in \mathbb{N}$ and $k \leq n$, the alternative A is chosen if the number of votes for A, which is defined as $|\{i : v_i = A\}|$, is greater than or equal to k, where v_i is the action chosen by voter i; the alternative B is chosen otherwise. Formally, define the voting rule $\Lambda_k : \times_{i \in I} V_i \to \{A, B\}$, such that

$$\Lambda_k(v) = \begin{cases} A & \text{if } |\{i : v_i = A\}| \geq k \\ B & \text{if } |\{i : v_i = A\}| < k, \end{cases}$$

for all action profiles v in $V = \times_{i \in I} V_i$. All voters are assumed to have the same ex-ante preferences, specifically $u(A, A) = u(B, B) = 1$ and $u(A, B) = u(B, A) = 0$, $\forall i \in I$. This concludes the definition of the voting game of Austen-Smith and Banks [1], which is denoted by $G = \langle I, \Theta, (T_i, V_i)_{i \in I}, u, \pi \rangle$.

A strategy for voter $i \in I$ in G is a function $\sigma_i : T_i \to \Delta(V_i)$. I denote $\sigma_i(v_i|t_i)$ as the probability that voter i chooses action $v_i \in V_i$ when observing $t_i \in T_i$. A strategy profile, defined as $\sigma = (\sigma_1, \ldots, \sigma_n) \in \Sigma$ and $\Sigma = \times_{i \in I} \Sigma_i$, is the set of strategy profiles in G. As is standard, denote by σ_{-i} the strategy profile $(\sigma_j)_{j \in I \setminus \{i\}}$, that is the strategy profile of all voters except i. Then, the common ex-ante expected payoff for each voter can be represented as $Eu(\theta, \Lambda_k(\sigma_1(t_1), \ldots, \sigma_n(t_n)))$, which is precisely the probability of a correct decision made by I when the strategy profile σ is used, given θ is the true state of the nature.

Given $\sigma \in \Sigma$, denote by $x_i(\sigma_i) : \Theta \times T_i \to \{0, 1\}$ the indicator variable of the set of correct voting of voter i, when using strategy σ_i, that is,

$$x_i(\sigma_i; \theta, t_i) = \begin{cases} 1 & \text{if } (\theta, v_i(t_i)) = (A, A) \text{ or } (\theta, v_i(t_i)) = (B, B) \\ 0 & \text{otherwise.} \end{cases}$$

Here, with a slight abuse of notation, further denote by $v_i(t_i)$ the realised pure action of i with type t_i, who uses strategy σ_i. Therefore, given σ, the probability distribution π on Ω induces a joint probability distribution defined over $X = \{x = (x_1, \ldots, x_n) \mid x_i \in \{0, 1\}\}$, which can be denoted by $\pi_\sigma(\theta, t)$. The random variable $f(\Lambda_k) : X \to \{0, 1\}$ associated with the given voting rule is

$$f(\Lambda_k; x(\sigma; \theta, t)) = \begin{cases} 1 & \text{if } (\theta, \Lambda_k(v_1(t_1), \ldots, v_n(t_n))) = (A, A) \text{ or } (\theta, \Lambda_k(v_1(t_1), \ldots, v_n(t_n))) = (B, B) \\ 0 & \text{otherwise.} \end{cases}$$

The random variable f partitions X into two mutually exclusive and exhaustive sets, X_{f_1} and $X_{f_0} = X \setminus X_{f_1}$, where $X_{f_1} = \{x \mid f(\Lambda_k; x) = 1\}$. Thus, the common ex-ante expected payoff for each voter under the voting rule Λ_k is given by $Eu = Pr(x \in X_{f_1})$.

Next, denote by $T_{-i}^{piv} = \{t_{-i} \in T_{-i} \mid |v_{-i}(t_{-i}) = A| = k - 1\}$ the type subprofile which, given strategy σ_{-i}, gives exactly $k-1$ votes of alternative A from all voters except i. In addition, denote by $T_{-i,f_1}^{piv} = \{t_{-i} \in T_{-i} \mid |v_{-i}(t_{-i}) = A| \neq k - 1 \text{ and } f(\Lambda_k; x_{-i}(\sigma_{-i}; \theta, t_{-i})) = 1\}$ the non-pivotal type subprofile of all voters except i, which leads to the collective decisions given strategy σ_{-i}.

Then, $X_{-i}^{piv} = \{x_{-i} = (x_j)_{j \in I \setminus \{i\}} \mid x_{-i} : \Theta \times T_{-i}^{piv} \to \{0, 1\}^{-i}\}$ is the set of all vectors of the random variables, which is defined over the pivotal voting profiles of all voters except i. Furthermore, $\overline{X_{-i,f_1}^{piv}} = \{x_{-i} \mid x_{-i} \notin X_{-i}^{piv} \text{ and } f(\Lambda_k; x_{-i}) = 1\}$ is the set of all vectors of the random variables that indicates the correct selected alternative, defined over the non-pivotal voting profiles of the $I \setminus \{i\}$ voters.

The ex-ante expected payoff can, thus, be rewritten as

$$Pr(x \in X_{f_1}) = Pr(x_i = 1, x_{-i} \in X_{-i}^{piv}) + Pr(x_{-i} \in X_{f_1}^{\overline{piv}}),$$

and, the interim expected utility of voter i given the private signal t_i, as

$$Pr(x \in X_{f_1}|t_i) = Pr(x_i = 1, x_{-i} \in X_{-i}^{piv}|t_i) + Pr(x_{-i} \in X_{-i,f_1}^{\overline{piv}}|t_i).$$

After receiving t_i, voter i updates their prior belief according to Bayes' rule, thereby forming the posterior belief π^{t_i} of the joint probability distribution of the states of the world. Next, denote the posterior belief by $\pi^{t_i}(\theta, t) = \pi^{t_i}(\theta) \times_{i \neq j} r_\theta(t_j)$. Then, the interim expected payoff for voter i, given strategy profile σ can be written as

$$Eu[\sigma_i, \sigma_{-i}|t_i] = \sum_{\theta \in \Theta} \sigma_i(\theta|t_i) \sum_{t_{-i} \in T_{-i}^{piv}} \pi_{\sigma_{-i}}^{t_i}(\theta, t_{-i}) + \sum_{t_{-i} \in T_{-i,f_1}^{\overline{piv}}} \pi_{\sigma_{-i}}^{t_i}(\theta, t_{-i}).$$

A Bayesian Nash equilibrium of G is a strategy profile $\sigma^* = (\sigma_1^*, \ldots, \sigma_n^*)$ such that for all $i \in I$, $Eu[\sigma_i^*, \sigma_{-i}^*|t_i] \geq Eu[\sigma_i, \sigma_{-i}^*|t_i]$ for every $t_i \in T_i$ and $\sigma_i \in \Sigma_i$, where $\sigma_{-i}^* = (\sigma_j^*)_{j \in I \setminus \{i\}}$. That is for all $\sigma_i \in \Sigma_i$,

$$\sum_{\theta \in \Theta} \sigma_i^*(\theta|t_i) \sum_{t_{-i} \in T_{-i}^{piv}} \pi_{\sigma_{-i}^*}^{t_i}(\theta, t_{-i}) + \sum_{t_{-i} \in T_{-i,f_1}^{\overline{piv}}} \pi_{\sigma_{-i}^*}^{t_i}(\theta, t_{-i}) \geq \sum_{\theta \in \Theta} \sigma_i(\theta|t_i) \sum_{t_{-i} \in T_{-i}^{piv}} \pi_{\sigma_{-i}^*}^{t_i}(\theta, t_{-i}) + \sum_{t_{-i} \in T_{-i,f_1}^{\overline{piv}}} \pi_{\sigma_{-i}^*}^{t_i}(\theta, t_{-i}) \quad (1)$$

$$\sum_{\theta \in \Theta} \sigma_i^*(\theta|t_i) \sum_{t_{-i} \in T_{-i}^{piv}} \pi_{\sigma_{-i}^*}^{t_i}(\theta, t_{-i}) \geq \sum_{\theta \in \Theta} \sigma_i(\theta|t_i) \sum_{t_{-i} \in T_{-i}^{piv}} \pi_{\sigma_{-i}^*}^{t_i}(\theta, t_{-i}). \quad (2)$$

Since $\pi(\theta, t_{-i})$ is a singleton so is each $\pi^{t_i}(\theta, t_{-i})$, and hence $\sum_{t_{-i} \in T_{-i,f_1}^{\overline{piv}}} \pi_{\sigma_{-i}^*}^{t_i}(\theta, t_{-i})$ in Equation (1), which implies Equation (2).

I denote by piv_i the event that voter i is pivotal, which is the case when $t_{-i} \in T_{-i}^{piv}$ given strategy profile σ_{-i}. Hence, the strategy profile $\sigma^* = (\sigma_1^*, \ldots, \sigma_n^*)$ is a Bayesian Nash Equilibrium of the game G if and only if for every $i \in I$ and every $t_i \in T_i$,

$$\sigma^* \in \underset{\sigma \in \Sigma}{\mathrm{argmax}} \sum_{\theta \in \Theta} \sigma_i(\theta|t_i) \pi_{\sigma_{-i}}^{t_i}(\theta, piv_i).$$

3. Pivotality in an Ambiguous Voting Model

In this section, I show the equilibrium condition for an ambiguous voting game, in which all players have a common set of priors $\Pi \subseteq \Delta(\Omega)$, which is a closed and convex set of probability distributions over the states of the world. I only look at the cases where the ambiguity regarding the structure of the game is embedded in the prior distribution. The ambiguity regarding each player's belief about their opponents' strategies is not considered.

The study of Kajii and Ui [14] proves the existence of the mixed strategy equilibrium of an incomplete information game with multiple priors, a tuple $\widehat{G} = \langle I, \Theta, (T_i, V_i, \Pi_i)_{i \in I}, \Phi, u \rangle$. In such a game, the incompleteness of the information is expressed by a non-empty compact set of priors Π_i over a finite set of payoff relevant states, the types T_i and the exogenously given updating rule Φ; and the action set V_i of each voter is assumed to be finite.

Given multiple priors, voters are no longer standard Bayesian players. For each $t_i \in T_i$ and $\pi_i \in \Pi_i$, denote by $\pi_i^{t_i} = \pi_i(\cdot|t_i)$ the conditional probability and by $\Pi_i^{t_i} = \{\pi_i^{t_i} \in \Delta(\Omega) \mid \pi_i \in \Pi_i\}$ the set of conditional probabilities over Ω. An updating rule $\Phi : T_i \to 2^{\Pi_i^{t_i}}$ indicates that for each $t_i \in T_i$, there is a non-empty compact subset of $\Pi_i^{t_i}$, i.e, the set of posterior probabilities $\Phi_i^{t_i}$.

The additional assumption is that players adopt the Maxmin decision rule of Gilboa and Schmeidler [10] implying that each player uses the least favourable posterior $\phi_i^{t_i} \in \Phi_i^{t_i}$ obtained from $\Phi(t_i)$ to evaluate their actions.

Therefore, a strategy profile $\sigma^* = (\sigma_1^*, \ldots, \sigma_n^*)$ is a Nash Equilibrium of the game $\hat{G}$ if and only if for every $i \in I$ and every $t_i \in T_i$,

$$\min_{\phi_i^{t_i} \in \Phi_i^{t_i}} Eu(\sigma_i^*(t_i), \sigma_{-i}^*|t_i) \geq \min_{\phi_i^{t_i} \in \Phi_i^{t_i}} Eu(\sigma_i(t_i), \sigma_{-i}^*|t_i),$$

for all $\sigma_i \in \Sigma_i$.

The voting game with a common set of priors is a special case of the game $\hat{G}$ proposed by Kajii and Ui [14]. In the proposed ambiguous voting game, the closed and convex set of priors are assumed to be common. In addition, the updating rule adopted by all Maxmin voters is the Full Bayesian Updating rule of Pires [15]. These two assumptions leads to the fact that $\Phi^{t_i} = \Pi^{t_i}$.

Hence, for the voting game $\tilde{G} = \langle I, \Theta, (T_i, V_i)_{i \in I}, \Pi, \Phi, u \rangle$, $\sigma^* = (\sigma_1^*, \ldots, \sigma_n^*)$ is a Nash Equilibrium if and only if for every $i \in I$ and every $t_i \in T_i$,

$$\sigma^* \in \underset{\sigma \in \Sigma}{\operatorname{argmax}} \min_{\pi^{t_i} \in \Pi^{t_i}} Eu(\sigma_i(t_i), \sigma_{-i}|t_i).$$

Next, I use the voting model of Ellis [8], which assumes ambiguity in the probability distribution over the states of the nature, and the voting model of Fabrizi et al. [9] [1], which assumes the ambiguous likelihood of the type distribution, as examples to prove the insufficiency of conditioning only on pivotality to establish the equilibrium condition for ambiguous voting games.

An Illustration: Ellis [8]

In the voting model of Ellis [8], there is a common set of priors Π, which is a closed and convex set of probability distributions over the states of the world, because the probability distribution of the state of nature is assumed to be ambiguous. In particular, the marginal probability of the state of nature A, denoted by

$$\pi(A) := \sum_{t \in T} \pi(A, t),$$

is between $\underline{p}$ and $\overline{p}$, where $0 < \underline{p} \leq \overline{p} < 1$, and

$$\pi(\theta, t) = \underset{i \in I}{\times} \pi(\theta, t_i) = \underset{i \in I}{\times} [\pi(t_j|\theta)\pi(\theta)] = \pi(\theta) \underset{i \in I}{\times} r_\theta(t_i),$$

for all $(\theta, t) \in \Omega$. Thus, for every $p \in [\underline{p}, \overline{p}]$, there exists

$$\pi(A, t) = p \underset{i \in I}{\times} r_A(t_i) \text{ and } \pi(B, t) = (1-p) \underset{i \in I}{\times} r_B(t_i).$$

Upon receiving t_i, voter i forms a set of posteriors $\Pi(\cdot|t_i)$ by updating each measure in Π. According to the updating rule Φ, the posterior probability $\pi^{t_i}(A)$ is between $\underline{p}^{t_i}$ and $\overline{p}^{t_i}$ so that

$$\pi^{t_i}(A, t) = p^{t_i} \underset{i \neq j}{\times} r_A(t_j) \text{ and } \pi^{t_i}(B, t) = (1 - p^{t_i}) \underset{i \neq j}{\times} r_B(t_j),$$

for every $p^{t_i} \in [\underline{p}^{t_i}, \overline{p}^{t_i}]$.

In addition, the voters have Maxmin preferences, which means that voter i evaluates strategy $\sigma_i(t_i)$ by the minimum probability of selecting the correct alternative.

---

[1] An earlier version of the paper by Fabrizi et al. [9] was circulated with the title "The good, the bad, and the not so ugly: Unanimity voting with ambiguous information".

Thus, the ambiguous voting game of Ellis [8] is defined by the game $\tilde{G} = \langle I, \Theta, (T_i, V_i)_{i \in I}, \Pi, \Phi, u \rangle$. The interim expected payoff to a strategy σ_i after $t_i \in T_i$, given $\sigma_{-i} \in \Sigma_{-i}$ is

$$U(\sigma_i(t_i), \sigma_{-i}|t_i) = \min_{\pi^{t_i} \in \Pi^{t_i}} Eu(\sigma_i(t_i), \sigma_{-i}|t_i)$$

$$= \min_{\pi^{t_i} \in \Pi^{t_i}} \sum_{\theta \in \Theta} \sigma_i(\theta|t_i) \left[\sum_{t_{-i} \in T^{piv}_{-i}} \pi^{t_i}_{\sigma_{-i}}(\theta, t_{-i}) + \sum_{t_{-i} \in T^{piv}_{-i, f_1}} \pi^{t_i}_{\sigma_{-i}}(\theta, t_{-i}) \right]$$

$$= \min_{\pi^{t_i}(\theta) \in \Pi^{t_i}(\theta)} \sum_{\theta \in \Theta} \pi^{t_i}(\theta) [\sigma_i(\theta|t_i) \sum_{t_{-i} \in T^{piv}_{-i}} \pi^{t_i}_{\sigma_{-i}}(t_{-i}) + \sum_{t_{-i} \in T^{piv}_{-i, f_1}} \pi^{t_i}_{\sigma_{-i}}(t_{-i})] \cdot \times$$

Then, for every $t_i \in T_i$ and every $\sigma_i \in \Sigma_i$,

$$U(\sigma_i^*(t_i), \sigma_{-i}^*|t_i) \geq U(\sigma_i(t_i), \sigma_{-i}^*|t_i),$$

if and only if

$$\min_{\pi^{t_i}(\theta) \in \Pi^{t_i}(\theta)} \sum_{\theta \in \Theta} \pi^{t_i}(\theta) [\sigma_i^*(\theta|t_i) \sum_{t_{-i} \in T^{piv}_{-i}} \pi^{t_i}_{\sigma_{-i}^*}(t_{-i}) + \sum_{t_{-i} \in T^{piv}_{-i, f_1}} \pi^{t_i}_{\sigma_{-i}^*}(t_{-i})]$$

$$\geq \min_{\pi^{t_i}(\theta) \in \Pi^{t_i}(\theta)} \sum_{\theta \in \Theta} \pi^{t_i}(\theta) [\sigma_i(\theta|t_i) \sum_{t_{-i} \in T^{piv}_{-i}} \pi^{t_i}_{\sigma_{-i}^*}(t_{-i}) + \sum_{t_{-i} \in T^{piv}_{-i, f_1}} \pi^{t_i}_{\sigma_{-i}^*}(t_{-i})]. \quad (3)$$

In Equation (3), as $\sigma_i^* \neq \sigma_i$, the posterior $\pi^{t_i}(\theta)$ which gives the minimum expected utility of choosing strategy σ_i^* might not necessarily be the one that leads to the minimum expected utility of choosing strategy σ_i. This simply shows that the probability that the correct alternative gets selected in the non-pivotal scenario cannot cancel out for this game $\tilde{G}$.

I denote by $\overline{piv}_{f_1}$ the event in which the correct alternative is selected by $I \setminus \{i\}$ voters. Then, Equation (3) implies that

$$\sigma^* \in \operatorname*{argmax}_{\sigma \in \Sigma} \min_{\pi^{t_i}(\theta) \in \Pi^{t_i}(\theta)} \sum_{\theta \in \Theta} \pi^{t_i}(\theta) [\sigma_i(\theta|t_i) \pi^{t_i}_{\sigma_{-i}}(piv) + \pi^{t_i}_{\sigma_{-i}}(\overline{piv}_{f_1})].$$

Another Illustration: Fabrizi et al. [9]

Another variation of the voting model is to assume that the probability distribution of the types conditional on the state of the nature is ambiguous. That is conditional on state θ, the signal that voter i gets is distributed according to one of the distributions in a closed and convex set R_θ, such that $r_A(a) = r_B(b) = \mu \in [\underline{\mu}, \overline{\mu}]$, where $1/2 < \underline{\mu} \leq \overline{\mu} < 1$. This forms a common set of priors Π over the states of the world such that $\pi \in \Pi$ if and only if there is a $\mu \in [\underline{\mu}, \overline{\mu}]$ so that $\pi(\theta, t) = \pi(\theta) \times_{i \in I} r_\theta(t_i)$, for all $(\theta, t) \in \Omega$. Hence, the voting game by Fabrizi et al. [9] can also be defined by $\tilde{G}$, except that the set of common priors is different from that of Ellis [8]. Consequently, both the pivotal and non-pivotal scenarios should be considered in the equilibrium condition of a voting game with ambiguity regarding the type distributions.

In each of the voting models discussed above, in spite of the different sources of the ambiguity, there exists a closed and convex set of common priors Π. Because the Full Bayesian Updating rule Φ is not singleton-valued, so is the set of posteriors $\Pi(\cdot|t_i)$. Hence, for Maxmin voters, the posteriors associated with different strategies are not necessarily the same, which precludes the possibility to eliminate the non-pivotal scenarios.

Therefore, a strategy profile σ^* is an equilibrium if and only if for every voter i of type t_i, it maximises their expected utility, given the posterior beliefs and that other voters follow the strategy profile σ_{-i}^*. That is, the minimum probability of the correct alternative, which encompasses the probability of voter i being pivotal and choosing the correct alternative, as well as the probability of voter i being non-pivotal, whereas $I \setminus \{i\}$ voters select the correct alternative, is maximised by σ^*.

I reiterate the main finding in the following proposition.

Proposition 1. *For the ambiguous voting game defined by $\tilde{G} = \langle I, \Theta, (T_i, V_i)_{i \in I}, \Pi, \Phi, u \rangle$, $\sigma^* = (\sigma_1^*, \ldots, \sigma_n^*)$ is the Nash Equilibrium if and only if for every $i \in I$ and every $t_i \in T_i$,*

$$\sigma^* \in \underset{\sigma \in \Sigma}{\arg\max} \min_{\pi^{t_i}(\theta) \in \Pi^{t_i}(\theta)} \sum_{\theta \in \Theta} \pi^{t_i}(\theta)[\sigma_i(\theta|t_i) \pi^{t_i}_{\sigma_{-i}}(piv) + \pi^{t_i}_{\sigma_{-i}}(\overline{piv}_{f_1})].$$

4. Conclusions

In this note, I provide simple derivations of the equilibrium conditions for voting games such as those of Austen-Smith and Banks [1] with a unique common prior, and Ellis [8] and Fabrizi et al. [9] with a set of common priors. I demonstrate that each voter cannot determine the best response merely based on the pivotal event. The non-pivotal events are also necessary components in the equilibrium condition whenever there is a common set of priors and an updating rule that is not singleton-valued.

The analysis is confined to the case where voters are Maxmin expected utility maximisers. This could be extended beyond the Maxmin preferences, for example, assuming voters are Choquet expected utility maximisers as in Schmeidler [16], who admit non-additive probabilities on the grand state space of the voting game under ambiguity. Extending the analysis of voting under ambiguity to more general classes of voter preferences, such as to CEU maximisers, would have its merits, but assuming CEU preferences would not change the core point of this note. Moreover, a similar decision-theoretical approach à la Eliaz, Ray, and Razin [11] can be applied to the ambiguous voting game to conduct the equilibrium analysis, and to compare choice shifts with the full information equivalence voting equilibrium. However, to address these points is beyond the scope of this note and is left for future research.

Funding: This research was funded by the Royal Society of New Zealand, Marsden Fund Standard Grant number UOA1617.

Acknowledgments: The author thanks Simona Fabrizi, John Hillas, John Panzar, Matthew Ryan, Ronald Stauber and audiences at the Centre for Mathematical Social Science research seminar for helpful comments. The initial idea for this note benefitted from conversations with Clemens Puppe and Arkadii Slinko. The author also thanks two anonymous referees and the editors for very useful comments on this note.

Conflicts of Interest: The author declares no conflict of interest. The funders had no role in the design of the study; in the collection, analyses, or interpretation of data; in the writing of the manuscript, or in the decision to publish the results.

References

1. Austen-Smith, D.; Banks, J.S. Information aggregation, rationality, and the Condorcet jury theorem. *Am. Political Sci. Rev.* **1996**, *90*, 34–45. [CrossRef]
2. Margolis, H. Pivotal voting. *J. Theor. Politics* **2001**, *13*, 111–116. [CrossRef]
3. Margolis, H. Game theory and juries: A miraculous result. *J. Theor. Politics* **2001**, *13*, 425–435. [CrossRef]
4. Margolis, H. Pivotal voting and the emperor's new clothes. *Soc. Choice Welf.* **2002**, *19*, 95–111. [CrossRef]
5. Dietrich, F.; Spiekermann, K. Epistemic democracy with defensible premises. *Econ. Philos.* **2013**, *29*, 87–120. [CrossRef]
6. Dietrich, F.; Spiekermann, K. Jury Theorems. Unpublished work, 2016.
7. Feddersen, T.; Pesendorfer, W. Convicting the innocent: The inferiority of unanimous jury verdicts under strategic voting. *Am. Political Sci. Rev.* **1998**, *92*, 23–35. [CrossRef]
8. Ellis, A. Condorcet meets Ellsberg. *Theor. Econ.* **2016**, *11*, 865–895. [CrossRef]
9. Fabrizi, S.; Lippert, S.; Pan, A.; Ryan, M. *Unanimous Jury Voting with an Ambiguous Likelihood*; University of Auckland: Auckland, New Zealand, 2019.
10. Gilboa, I.; Schmeidler, D. Maxmin expected utility with non-unique prior. *J. Math. Econ.* **1989**, *18*, 141–153. [CrossRef]
11. Eliaz, K.; Ray, D.; Razin, R. Choice shifts in groups: A decision-theoretic basis. *Am. Econ. Rev.* **2006**, *96*, 1321–1332. [CrossRef]

12. Dillenberger, D.; Raymond, C. On the Consensus Effect. Unpublished work, 2019.
13. Quiggin, J. A theory of anticipated utility. *J. Econ. Behav. Organ.* **1982**, *3*, 323–343. [CrossRef]
14. Kajii, A.; Ui, T. Incomplete information games with multiple priors. *Jpn. Econ. Rev.* **2005**, *56*, 332–351. [CrossRef]
15. Pires, C.P. A rule for updating ambiguous beliefs. *Theory Decis.* **2002**, *53*, 137–152. [CrossRef]
16. Schmeidler, D. Subjective probability and expected utility without additivity. *Econometrica* **1989**, *57*, 571–587. [CrossRef]

© 2019 by the author. Licensee MDPI, Basel, Switzerland. This article is an open access article distributed under the terms and conditions of the Creative Commons Attribution (CC BY) license (http://creativecommons.org/licenses/by/4.0/).

Article
A Game-Free Microfoundation of Mutual Optimism

Marco Serena

Max Planck Institute for Tax Law and Public Finance, Department of Public Economics, Marstallplatz 1, D-80539 München, Germany; marco.serena@tax.mpg.de

Received: 11 July 2019; Accepted: 25 September 2019; Published: 27 September 2019

Abstract: One of the most widely accepted explanations for why wars occur despite its Pareto-suboptimality is mutual optimism: if both sides expect to gain a lot by fighting, war becomes inevitable. The literature on mutual optimism typically assumes mutually optimistic beliefs and shows that, under such an assumption, war may occur despite its Pareto-suboptimality. In a war–peace model, we show that, if players neglect the correlation between other players' actions and their types—a well-established concept in economics—then players' expected payoffs from war increase relative to conventional informational sophistication predictions, hence providing a microfoundation of mutual optimism.

Keywords: mutual optimism; incentives to go to war; information; correlation neglect

1. Introduction

If rational country leaders have mutually consistent beliefs about the outcome of a costly war, then a bargain in which Pareto improves upon war must be reachable. The lack of mutually consistent beliefs is an often mentioned rationalist explanation for war. As reported by Slantchev and

> If both sides expect to gain a lot by fighting—perhaps because both expect to win with near certainty at an acceptably low cost—then [...] war becomes the inevitable outcome. This argument is now generally known as the *mutual optimism* explanation of war and is among the most widely accepted explanations of why war occurs.

Due to mutual optimism, both players may expect to be better off going to war even if a war would shrink the players' aggregate payoff. Pioneers of this idea are the seminal works by Wittman (1979) [2] and Blainey (1988) [3], and a number of scholars have contributed to the idea (e.g., Morrow, 1989 [4]; Fearon, 1995 [5]; Werner, 1998 [6]; Wagner, 2000 [7]; Slantchev and Tarar, 2011) [1]. This strand of the literature typically *assumes* mutual optimism in war–peace models and concludes that mutual optimism enhances the incentives to go to war: "it could be that two states each are optimistic and are convinced that they will benefit from a war. In these cases war can erupt, as long as the inconsistency of beliefs is large enough to compensate for the cost of war" (Jackson and Morelli, 2011) [8]. In the present paper, we provide a microfoundation for mutual optimism: namely, we show that mutual optimism arises when players correctly predict the distribution of other players' actions and types but—in contrast to informational sophistication—draw no inference about the correlation between the two.[1]

Such informational naivety of players has a long and prosperous history in economics: pioneered, among others, by Kagel and Levin (1986) [9] and Holt and Sherman (1994) [10], it has been extended along several directions. For instance, informational naivety is a special case of cursed equilibria (Eyster

---

[1] In line with orthodox economic terminology, type refers to payoff-relevant parameters.

and Rabin, 2005) [11], analogy-based expectation equilibria (Jehiel, 2005) [12], and self-confirming equilibria (Fudenberg and Levine, 1993) [13].[2] Hence, the informational naivety of the present paper reaches out to all those concepts. Since, to the best of our knowledge, there is no unique undisputed terminology for the correlation neglect between other players' actions and types, we choose the neutral though novel term informational naivety."

We incorporate informational naivety of players into a war–peace model. The main result of the paper is to show that informational naivety increases players' expected payoffs from war relative to informational sophistication predictions, thus microfounding mutual optimism.

The following stylized version of our war–peace model illustrates the role of informational naivety. Each of the two players has resources (types) independently drawn from a prior distribution. A player privately knows their own resources but ignores the amount of resources of the other. Under peace, players consume their own resources, but if a war breaks out, the winner obtains the total resources and the loser obtains 0.[3] One common modeling approach is that a player, upon observing their own resources, chooses their level of military action, which increases their probability of winning a prospective war. However, since many war–peace models predict a positive equilibrium relation between a player's resources and their military action, one could sidestep the explicit modeling of military actions and directly assume that a player's probability of victory *increases* in their resources. We make this monotonicity assumption in the main part of the present paper (until Section 6), since for our purposes, we are not interested in players' choice of military actions but in the characterization of players' expected payoffs from war with and without informational naivety. This monotonicity assumption, named (*MonProb*) in the model (see Section 3), is both common in the literature and empirically sound.[4] Superimposing to the present model an endogenous military action which fulfills the abovementioned monotonicities would thus not affect our result. In fact, Section 7 endogenizes efforts, confirms the result of the previous sections, and derives comparative statics.

Therefore, as we do not model military actions explicitly, we implement informational naivety as neglecting the correlation between types and the result of strategic interactions yielding a certain probability of victory. In particular, an informationally naïve player correctly predicts the distribution of possible levels of resources of their rival and of the possible probabilities of victory, but in contrast to informational sophistication, they draws no inference about the correlation between the two: in other words, an informationally naïve player fails to infer the *mapping* from each possible level of resource of their rival to their corresponding probability of victory. We show that this failure systematically *increases* players' expected payoffs from war; that is, informational naivety microfounds mutual optimism.

Section 2 analyses the most stylized example of our model capable of capturing our result and explains its simple intuition. Sections 3 and 4 provide a formal generalization of the example in Section 2. Section 5 discusses four further extensions. Section 6 discusses the model's lack of choice

---

[2] In a cursed equilibrium, players draw *partial* inference about the correlation between other players' actions and their types. Informational naivety is the *fully* cursed equilibrium, whereby no inference is drawn. Informational naivety is also a special case of an analogy-based expectation equilibria, where players' analogy partitions coincide with their own information partitions (see Eyster and Rabin, 2010, p. 1634 [14]; Jehiel and Koessler, 2007, p. 539 [15]; and Ettinger and Jehiel, 2010 [16], footnote 7). Finally, informational naivety is a special case of self-confirming equilibria, where the cursed players observe only the aggregate play of the opponents and neither the state nor the opponent's type (Fudenberg, 2006) [17]. The three concepts differ in how they convexify informational naivety and informational sophistication. Since we focus only on these two extremes, we do not need to take a stand among the three concepts.

[3] In the general model of Section 3, we will only adopt the weaker assumption, (*MonSpoils*), that the spoils of war increase in the rival's resources.

[4] For instance, Jackson and Morelli (2007) [18] assume that the probability of winning the war satisfies (*MonProb*) without explicitly modeling the arming phase. Bueno de Mesquita (1981, p. 102) [19] also assumes that wealth translates into military capability. Hörner et al.'s (2015) [20] workhorse model has two types, h and l, and probabilities satisfy $p_{h,l} > 1/2 = p_{h,h} = p_{l,l} > p_{l,h}$, consistent with (*MonProb*). Taking types as sunk military investments, Meirowitz and Sartori (2008) [21] assume (*MonProb*). Furthermore, (*MonProb*) typically arises in conflict models with resource constraints, such as Tullock contests and Colonel Blotto games. For empirical evidence supporting (*MonProb*), see, for instance, footnote 15 in Jackson and Morelli (2007) [18] and the references therein.

variables for players. Conversely, Section 7 analyses a simple model where players choose efforts and derives comparative statics. Section 8 discusses our result.

2. A Stylized Example and the Intuition

In order to spell out the intuition, we present the most stylized nontrivial example of the model of Section 3.

Each of the two players privately knows their own resources, which are either high ($R > 0$) or low (0) with equal probability.[5] Under peace, each player consumes their own resources. Under war, the winner obtains the total amount of resources minus the costs of war $c \geq 0$ and the loser obtains 0.[6] When a war is between players with equal resources, each has a 1/2 probability of winning. When a war is between players with unequal resources, the player with resources R has a probability of winning equal to $p \in (1/2, 1]$. This specification is consistent with (MonProb): win probabilities increase in one's own type.

Under informational sophistication (IS), a player with resource R expects to be better off under war than peace when

$$\pi_{IS}^R \equiv \frac{1}{2}\left[\frac{1}{2}(2R-c)\right] + \frac{1}{2}[p(R-c)] \geq R. \tag{1}$$

With probability 1/2, a player with resources R is up against a rival also with resources R, so that they have a 1/2 probability of winning, $2R - c$ (the total resources minus the costs of war), while with probability 1/2, a player with resources R is up against a player with 0 resources, so that they have probability p of winning $R - c$ (the total resources minus the costs of war).

Under informational naivety (IN), a player with resources R expects to be better off under war than peace when

$$\pi_{IN}^R \equiv \left(\frac{1}{2}\frac{1}{2} + \frac{1}{2}p\right)\left(\frac{1}{2}2R + \frac{1}{2}R - c\right) \geq R. \tag{2}$$

Despite an informationally naïve player correctly perceiving their average probability of victory (first bracket of Equation (2)) and their average spoils of war (second bracket of Equation (2)), they draw no inference about the correlation between the two.

An IN player differs from an IS player in that they fail to understand that high spoils of war ($2R$) bring along the bad news that their probability of victory is only 1/2 rather than $p \in (1/2, 1]$ and that low spoils of war (R) bring along the good news that their probability of victory is $p \in (1/2, 1]$. These two forces go in the same direction: an IN player with resources R overestimates their expected payoff from war relative to an IS player. Formally, $\pi_{IN}^R > \pi_{IS}^R$ for every parameter triple (R, c, p).[7] The same holds for an IN player with resources 0: $\pi_{IN}^0 > \pi_{IS}^0$ for every parameter triple (R, c, p).[8] In words, informational naivety increases a player's expected payoff from war relative to informational sophistication predictions.

Despite the main point of the paper being that $\pi_{IN}^R > \pi_{IS}^R$ and $\pi_{IN}^0 > \pi_{IS}^0$, it may still be of interest to analyse when players are better off under war than under peace. Trivial algebra gives the threshold for c below which a player is better off under war:

---

[5] The normalization of low resources to 0 is qualitatively innocuous.
[6] The result would carry over if the costs of war $c \geq 0$ depend on players' resources or are paid by both players rather than only by the winner. Similarly, the normalization of the loser's payoff to 0 is without loss of generality, and for simplicity, the normalization is maintained throughout the paper.
[7] Peace payoffs depend on resources but not on probabilities of victory and are thus unaffected by informational naivety.
[8] The conditions corresponding to Equations (1) and (2) for a player with 0 resources read as follows:

$$\pi_{CGT}^0 \equiv \frac{1}{2}\left[\frac{1}{2}(-c)\right] + \frac{1}{2}[(1-p)(R-c)] \geq 0$$

$$\pi_{IN}^0 \equiv \left(\frac{1}{2}\frac{1}{2} + \frac{1}{2}(1-p)\right)\left(\frac{1}{2}R - c\right) \geq 0$$

From Table 1, we can draw a number of conclusions. If the costs of war are overwhelmingly high, peace is the unique outcome of virtually all standard war-declaration models superimposed on the above payoff structure, since both players are strictly better off under peace. Similarly, overwhelmingly low costs of war yield a war to break out. The predictions are more interesting when costs are intermediate, where war is sustained according to resources and informational naivety (IN). Since $c_0^{IS} < c_0^{IN}$, there is an intermediate range of costs, $c \in [c_0^{IS}, c_0^{IN}]$, where a 0-resource player prefers war than peace under IN but not under IS. Similarly, since $c_R^{IS} < c_R^{IN}$, when $c \in [c_R^{IS}, c_R^{IN}]$, an R-resource player prefers war than peace under IN but not under IS.[9] Although the above example is highly stylized, it outlines the main insight of this paper: informational naivety increases a player's expected payoff from war relative to informational sophistication predictions.

Table 1. Threshold of c below which a player expects to be better off under war than peace.

Better off under war if	R-Resource Player	0-Resource Player
Informational Sophistication	$c \leq \frac{2(p-1)}{2p+1} R \equiv c_R^{IS}$	$c \leq \frac{2(p-1)}{2p-3} R \equiv c_0^{IS}$
Informational Naïveté	$c \leq \frac{6p-5}{4p+2} R \equiv c_R^{IN}$	$c \leq \frac{1}{2} R \equiv c_0^{IN}$

The stylized example has been conceived under (i) distribution of types, which is uniform, binary, and symmetric across players; (ii) spoils of war, which equal the sum of types minus the fixed cost of war; and (iii) probabilities of victory taking values $1/2$, p, or $1 - p$. However, the result of the stylized example is no coincidence, and Sections 3 and 4 generalize it to (i) possibly nonuniform n-type asymmetric distribution of types, (ii) spoils of war decreasing in rival's type, and (iii) probability of victory increasing in one's own type.

3. The Model

Each of the two risk-neutral players privately observes their own type; in particular, the first (or second) player's type is drawn from a distribution, which assigns probability $r_i \in [0,1]$ ($q_i \in [0,1]$) to each type θ_i with $i \in \Theta \equiv \{1,..,n\}$ and $\sum_{i \in \Theta} r_i = 1$ ($\sum_{i \in \Theta} q_i = 1$). This specification allows players' type distributions to possibly differ in probabilities and supports (e.g., setting $r_1 > 0 = q_1$ makes type θ_1 possible only for the first player). Without loss of generality, assume that $\theta_1 < \theta_2 < .. < \theta_n$, and we refer to type θ_n as the strongest (wealthiest) type. We compare two alternative settings: peace, $\mathcal{P}$, and war, $\mathcal{W}$.

Under $\mathcal{P}$, we denote player i's payoff under peace by $\pi_i^\mathcal{P}(\theta_i, \theta_j)$. If types are resource levels (e.g., territory, GDP, and technology), as in the example in Section 2, $\pi_i^\mathcal{P}(\theta_i, \theta_j) = \theta_i$; that is, under peace, a player consumes their own resources. We do not need to specify how $\pi_i^\mathcal{P}$ depends on types: thus, for instance, we allow for spillovers across types as well as different returns to types.

Under $\mathcal{W}$, players engage in a war. If player i loses, their payoff is 0. If player i wins, their payoff is $\pi_i^\mathcal{W}(\theta_i, \theta_j) \equiv f(\theta_i, \theta_j) > 0$. As discussed, one's spoils of war increase in the rival's type. Formally,

$(MonSpoils): f(\theta_i, \theta_j)$ strictly increases in θ_j for each θ_i.

The interpretation of $(MonSpoils)$ clearly depends on the interpretation of type. If types are resource levels, as in our leading example, players engage in a resource war, and $(MonSpoils)$ says that the richer the defeated rival, the greater the spoils of war. A special case is that the winner obtains the total resources, possibly with destructiveness parameters $d_1, d_2 \in [0,1]$ and/or a cost of

---

[9] Notice that, while for 0-resource players, $0 \leq c_0^{IS} < c_0^{IN}$, for R-resource players, $c_R^{IS} \leq 0$ and $c_R^{IN} \geq 0 \iff p \geq 5/6$. Hence, while the intermediate range of costs always exists for 0-resource players, it may not exist for R-resource players.

war $c \geq 0$;[10] that is, $f(\theta_i, \theta_j) = d_1\theta_i + d_2\theta_j - c$.[11] In Section 2, we discussed $d_1 = d_2 = 1$. Alternatively, one could interpret types as military proficiencies, troop qualities, or political resolves: the benefit of war obtained by a player who defeats a stronger or more resolute rival than themself is in terms of glory or reputational gains and, thus, depends positively on the rival's type and negatively on one's own type: for instance, $f(\theta_i, \theta_j) = \theta_j - \theta_i$ or $f(\theta_i, \theta_j) = \theta_j/\theta_i$.

Furthermore, we assume that, in case of war $\mathcal{W}$, a player's probability of victory increases in their own type. Formally, if we denote by $p_i(\theta_i, \theta_j)$ the probability of winning the war of a player of type θ_i up against a player of type θ_j, then we impose the following monotonicity assumption:[12]

$$(MonProb): p_i(\theta_i, \theta_j) \text{ strictly increases in } \theta_i \text{ for each } \theta_j.$$

Exactly one of the two players wins the war: if players are of types θ_i and θ_j, then $p_i(\theta_i, \theta_j) + p_j(\theta_j, \theta_i) = 1$. An immediate consequence of this fact, together with $(MonProb)$, is that a player's probability of victory strictly decreases in their rival's type: $p_i(\theta_i, \theta_j)$ strictly decreases in θ_j.

If types are resource levels, as in our leading example, $(MonProb)$ echoes, for instance, Jackson and Morelli (2007) [18] and the papers discussed in footnote 4. An examples of conflict technology consistent with $(MonProb)$ is the Tullock success function, where $p_i(\theta_i, \theta_j) = \theta_i/(\theta_i + \theta_j)$. However, our main result, much as the majority of Jackson and Morelli's (2007) [18] results, do not depend on which specific conflict technology is chosen as long as $(MonProb)$ is fulfilled.

4. The Main Result

As $\pi_i^P(\theta_i, \theta_j)$ depends on types but not on probabilities of victory, a player's expected payoff under peace is identical under IN and IS. Therefore, we exclusively focus on whether and how players' expected payoffs from war vary between IN and IS.

Proposition 1. *Assume $(MonProb)$ and $(MonSpoils)$. A player's expected payoff from war is strictly greater when they are informationally naïve than under informational sophistication.*

Proof of Proposition 1. We want to show that $E_{IN}[\pi_t^\mathcal{W}] - E_{IS}[\pi_t^\mathcal{W}] > 0$. Let the first player's type be a generic θ_t: their probability of winning a war is $p_t(\theta_t, \theta_i)$ when up against a θ_i rival. Indeces i, j, and k will be used interchangeably throughout the algebraic steps below.

The difference of expected payoffs from war for the first player of generic type θ_t under IN and IS is positive if

$$E_{IN}[\pi_t^\mathcal{W}] - E_{IS}[\pi_t^\mathcal{W}] > 0,$$

$$\left[\sum_{j=1}^n q_j p_t(\theta_t, \theta_j)\right]\left[\sum_{k=1}^n q_k f(\theta_t, \theta_k)\right] - \sum_{i=1}^n q_i p_t(\theta_t, \theta_i) f(\theta_t, \theta_i) > 0, \quad (3)$$

$$\sum_{i=1}^n q_i f(\theta_t, \theta_i)\left[\sum_{j=1}^n q_j p_t(\theta_t, \theta_j) - p_t(\theta_t, \theta_i)\right] > 0,$$

---

[10] An interpretation is that, if a player wins, they gain only a fixed fraction of the rival's resources, as assumed, for instance, by Jackson and Morelli (2007) [18].
[11] Throughout the paper, we omit, for the sake of space, the dependence of $f(\theta_i, \theta_j)$ on any variable different than types. Recall, however, that $f(\theta_i, \theta_j)$ may depend on any number of other parameters, such as, in the examples spelled out so far, the destructiveness parameters d_1, d_2, and the cost of war c.
[12] Note that we allow for $p(\theta_i, \theta_i) \neq 1/2$. As pointed out by Jackson and Morelli (2007) [18], "[T]his allows i, for instance, to have some geographic, population, or technological advantage or disadvantage."

and since $\forall i \in \Theta$, there is a $j \in \Theta$ such that $i = j$ and we can take $p_t(\theta_t, \theta_j)$ outside the running sum of js and obtain

$$\sum_{i=1}^{n} q_i f(\theta_t, \theta_i) \left[\sum_{j \neq i} q_j p_t(\theta_t, \theta_j) + (q_i - 1) p_t(\theta_t, \theta_i) \right] > 0,$$

$$\sum_{i=1}^{n} q_i f(\theta_t, \theta_i) \left[\sum_{j \neq i} q_j p_t(\theta_t, \theta_j) - \sum_{k \neq i} q_k p_t(\theta_t, \theta_i) \right] > 0,$$

since $q_i - 1 = -\sum_{k \neq i} q_k$. Collecting qs, we obtain

$$\sum_{i=1}^{n} q_i f(\theta_t, \theta_i) \left[\sum_{j \neq i} q_j \left(p_t(\theta_t, \theta_j) - p_t(\theta_t, \theta_i) \right) \right] > 0.$$

In the above expression, the sign of $p_t(\theta_t, \theta_j) - p_t(\theta_t, \theta_i)$ depends on $j \lessgtr i$; thus, we cannot yet conclude the left-hand-side positivity. However, we can rewrite the above expression as follows:[13]

$$\sum_{i=1}^{n} q_i f(\theta_t, \theta_i) \left[\sum_{j=i+1}^{n} q_j \left(p_t(\theta_t, \theta_j) - p_t(\theta_t, \theta_i) \right) + \sum_{j=1}^{i-1} q_j \left(p_t(\theta_t, \theta_j) - p_t(\theta_t, \theta_i) \right) \right] > 0,$$

$$\sum_{i=1}^{n} q_i f(\theta_t, \theta_i) \left[\sum_{j=i+1}^{n} q_j \left(p_t(\theta_t, \theta_j) - p_t(\theta_t, \theta_i) \right) - \sum_{j=1}^{i-1} q_j \left(p_t(\theta_t, \theta_i) - p_t(\theta_t, \theta_j) \right) \right] > 0,$$

$$\sum_{i=1}^{n} \sum_{j=i+1}^{n} q_i q_j f(\theta_t, \theta_i) \left(p_t(\theta_t, \theta_j) - p_t(\theta_t, \theta_i) \right)$$

$$- \sum_{i=1}^{n} \sum_{j=1}^{i-1} q_i q_j f(\theta_t, \theta_i) \left(p_t(\theta_t, \theta_i) - p_t(\theta_t, \theta_j) \right) > 0.$$

For all pairs (i, j) of the first double summation, there exists a unique pair of the second double summation with i and j swapped, and vice versa: e.g., when $(i, j) = (2, 4)$ in the first double summation, there exists an element with $(i, j) = (4, 2)$ in the second double summation, and vice versa. In fact, the number of elements is $n(n-1)/2$ in both double summations. Therefore, we can merge the two double summations into the following expression:

$$\sum_{i=1}^{n} \sum_{j=i+1}^{n} q_i q_j \left[f(\theta_t, \theta_i) - f(\theta_t, \theta_j) \right] \left[p_t(\theta_t, \theta_j) - p_t(\theta_t, \theta_i) \right] > 0. \quad (4)$$

Since $j > i$, $\theta_j > \theta_i$, and thus by (*MonSpoils*) and (*MonProb*), all elements of the summation of Equation (4) are strictly positive, being the product of two strictly negative elements. This proves Equation (4) and, thus, concludes the proof for the second player. The analogous proof works considering the payoffs of the second player of generic θ_t by simply replacing qs with rs in the above steps. In fact, the informational naivety or informational sophistication of a player does *not* affect the other player's expected payoff and, hence, the other player's incentive to declare war. □

5. Extensions

More than two players. When players have more than one rival, both (*MonProb*) and (*MonSpoils*) can be promptly generalized by redefining θ_j as the vector of rivals' types; that is, is probability of

---

[13] Notice that, when $i = n$ ($i = 1$), the first (second) summation within the square bracket is null.

victory decreases and the spoils of war increase in *any* rival's type. Under such generalized assumptions, Proposition 1 carries over. Such a generalization would add extra weight to the notation and would come at a cost of space without adding much insight, and thus, we omit its formal analysis.

Interior informational naivety. IN players fully neglect the correlation between rival's actions and types. A handy concept to capture partial neglect is that of partial cursedness (see Eyster and Rabin, 2005) [11]. Denoting by $\chi \in [0,1]$, the cursedness parameter, $\chi = 0$ corresponds to IS and $\chi = 1$ corresponds to IN. The expected payoff from war of a player affected by general cursedness $\chi \in [0,1]$ and of type θ_t is as follows:

$$\chi \left[\sum_{j=1}^n q_j p_t(\theta_t, \theta_j)\right] \left[\sum_{k=1}^n q_k f(\theta_t, \theta_k)\right] + (1-\chi)\sum_{i=1}^n q_i p_t(\theta_t, \theta_i) f(\theta_t, \theta_i), \tag{5}$$

The expected payoff increases in χ if and only if Equation (3) holds: hence, players' expected payoffs from war increase in the cursedness parameter χ, thus generalizing the result of Proposition 1.

Weakening (*MonProb*) **and** (*MonSpoils*). We required $f(\theta_i, \theta_j)$ to strictly increase in θ_j and $p_i(\theta_i, \theta_j)$ to strictly increase in θ_i. This guarantees that *every* element of Equation (4) is strictly positive. Nevertheless, it suffices that $f(\theta_i, \theta_j)$ and $p_i(\theta_i, \theta_j)$ weakly increase and that both strictly increase for at least one pair of types, so as to have that Equation (4) holds with strictinequality.[14]

Type-contingent expected payoff from war. In the stylized example of Section 2, the increase due to IN in a player's expected payoff from war is identical for 0- and R-resource players; that is, $\pi_{IN}^0 - \pi_{IS}^0 = \pi_{IN}^R - \pi_{IS}^R$. However, in the general setting of Section 3, this is not necessarily true. Following the steps of the proof of Proposition 1 leading to Equation (4), we can conclude that $E_{IN}[\pi_t^W] - E_{IS}[\pi_t^W]$ strictly decreases (increases) in θ_t if and only if, for all types t,

$$\sum_{i=1}^n \sum_{j=i+1}^n q_i q_j \left[f(\theta_{t+1}, \theta_i) - f(\theta_{t+1}, \theta_j)\right] \left[p_{t+1}(\theta_{t+1}, \theta_j) - p_{t+1}(\theta_{t+1}, \theta_i)\right] > (<) \tag{6}$$

$$\sum_{i=1}^n \sum_{j=i+1}^n q_i q_j \left[f(\theta_t, \theta_i) - f(\theta_t, \theta_j)\right] \left[p_t(\theta_t, \theta_j) - p_t(\theta_t, \theta_i)\right].$$

However, (*MonProb*) and (*MonSpoils*) do not suffice to shed light on the sign of Equation (6). One simple way to do so is by assuming strict supermodularity or submodularity of spoils f and probabilities p;[15] that is, the marginal benefit (in terms of spoils or probability) of defeating a rival of higher type increases in one's own type. The stylized example of Section 2, where $f(\theta_i, \theta_j) = \theta_i + \theta_j - c$, is the knife-edge case of modular spoils.[16]

6. Game-Free Model

The comparison of players' expected payoffs from war under informational sophistication and informational naivety sufficed to microfound mutual optimism. However, a common approach is to model players' choice between war and peace, among others, as endogenous and to characterize the equilibria of such a game. In this section, we discuss the pros and cons of the two approaches: our game-free" approach and the alternative game-idiosyncratic approach, where players have choice variables and where equilibria are derived.

---

[14] The all-pay auction technology, where $p_i(\theta_i, \theta_j) = 1$ when $\theta_i > \theta_j$, $p_i(\theta_i, \theta_j) = 0$ when $\theta_i < \theta_j$, and $p_i(\theta_i, \theta_j) = 1/2$ when $\theta_i = \theta_j$, satisfies the weakening of (*MonProb*), but for some pairs of types, it may not satisfy the original (*MonProb*).

[15] The function $f : \Theta^2 \to \Re$ satisfies strict supermodularity in (θ_i, θ_j) if $f(\theta_i', \theta_j') - f(\theta_i', \theta_j) > f(\theta_i, \theta_j') - f(\theta_i, \theta_j)$ for any $\theta_i' > \theta_i$ and $\theta_j' > \theta_j$. Strict submodularity is similarly defined.

[16] Knife-edge as $f(\theta_i', \theta_j') - f(\theta_i', \theta_j) = f(\theta_i, \theta_j') - f(\theta_i, \theta_j)$.

Our game-free approach has a number of advantages. First, the results derived in a game-free model are not an artifact of a particular game form. Second, our game-free model encompassed the concept of informational naivety in players' expected payoffs, sidestepping the need to characterize equilibria. Third, and most importantly, in our game-free model, we do not need to take a stand on many rather controversial modeling issues. An example is whether the conflict is unilateral or bilateral, that is, whether one side could be forced to fight even if it wished to avoid the conflict or whether the conflict occurs only if both sides choose to stand firm. Examples of models with unilateral conflicts are Powell (1993) [22], Jackson and Morelli (2007) [18], and Slantchev and Tarar (2011) [1] and that with bilateral conflicts are Bueno de Mesquita and Lalman (1992) [23], Fearon (1994) [24], and Fey and Ramsay (2007) [25]. Other examples are the timing of the game, the specific way war is destructive or costly, players' choice variables (e.g., military expenditure or choice to declare war), or the conflict technology (e.g., whether the probability of victory is proportional to ratios or differences of military efforts).

Nevertheless, working with a game-free model comes at a cost: we cannot derive testable predictions concerning players' behavior. Superimposing a game to our model would yield more specific and case-by-case predictions and comparative statics. In this sense, a game-idiosyncratic approach would complement our game-free approach.

In the trade-off between the generality of the model and the resulting testable predictions concerning players' behavior, we opted for the first so as to test the reach of our microfoundation exercise. Nevertheless, in the next section, we analyse a simple game-idiosyncratic model, where players' efforts are endogenous, and we derive comparative statics on efforts, so as to complement our game-free model.

7. Game-Idiosyncratic Model

While, so far, we focused on informational considerations, in this section, we address strategic considerations more explicitly. In particular, we explicitly model efforts denoted by e_i^j for player $i \in \{1,2\}$ with resources $j \in \{0, R\}$ as a choice variable, and the individual probability of victory is modeled à la Tullock; that is, player i's probability of victory equals their own effort divided by the total effort.[17] Both under IS and IN, we analyse type-symmetric equilibria; that is, if the two players have the same level of resources, they exert the same equilibrium level of effort—i.e., $e_1^0 = e_2^0 \equiv e^0$ and $e_1^R = e_2^R \equiv e^R$.

In this setting with endogenous effort and Tullock conflict, we maintain the fixed costs paid by the winner as in the model of Section 2 (i.e., $f(\theta_i, \theta_j) = \theta_i + \theta_j - c$) but we additionally assume that, regardless of the outcome of the war, each player pays a cost of effort equal to the effort exerted by that player.

7.1. Informational Sophistication

Under IS, the expected payoffs from war of a player with resources R and 0, respectively, equal[18]

$$\frac{1}{2}\frac{e_1^R}{e_1^R + e_2^R}(2R - c) + \frac{1}{2}\frac{e_1^R}{e_1^R + e_2^0}(R - c) - e_1^R \text{ and } \frac{1}{2}\frac{e_1^0}{e_1^0 + e_2^R}(R - c) + \frac{1}{2}\frac{e_1^0}{e_1^0 + e_2^0}(-c) - e_1^0.$$

If $c = 0$, routine maximization steps yield the unique type-symmetric equilibrium:

$$e^0 = \frac{-1 + \sqrt{5}}{16} \text{ and } e^R = \frac{3 + \sqrt{5}}{16}. \tag{7}$$

---

[17] If both players exert 0 effort, each player has 1/2 probability of victory.
[18] Throughout this subsection and the next one, we spell out the maximization problem of player 1. That of player 2 is symmetric.

If $c \in [R, 2R]$, we immediately obtain $e_1^0 = e_2^0 = 0$ from the maximization problem of a player with resources 0, and plugging this result into the FOC of a player with resources R gives the following unique type-symmetric equilibrium:

$$e^0 = 0 \text{ and } e^R = \frac{2R-c}{8}. \tag{8}$$

For intermediate values of c, obtaining a closed-form solution for equilibrium efforts is challenging, and in fact, there are two interior type-symmetric equilibria. However, even without closed-form solution, one can easily prove that, in any interior equilibrium, the following property holds.

Lemma 1. *If $c \in (0, R)$, in an interior type-symmetric equilibrium of the game under IS, $e^R > e^0$.*

Proof. Assume by contradiction that $e^0 \geq e^R$. The FOCs for the two types of player 1 read,[19]

$$FOC_1^R \; : \; \frac{1}{2}\frac{e_2^R}{(e_1^R + e_2^R)^2}(2R-c) + \frac{1}{2}\frac{e_2^0}{(e_1^R + e_2^0)^2}(R-c) = 1,$$

$$FOC_1^0 \; : \; \frac{1}{2}\frac{e_2^R}{(e_1^0 + e_2^R)^2}(R-c) + \frac{1}{2}\frac{e_2^0}{(e_1^0 + e_2^0)^2}(-c) = 1,$$

and the FOCs for the two types of player 2 are symmetric. Applying type-symmetry, we obtain

$$FOC^R \; : \; \frac{1}{8e^R}(2R-c) + \frac{1}{2}\frac{e^0}{(e^R + e^0)^2}(R-c) = 1,$$

$$FOC^0 \; : \; \frac{1}{2}\frac{e^R}{(e^0 + e^R)^2}(R-c) + \frac{1}{8e^0}(-c) = 1,$$

and considering the ratio of the addends containing the term with $(R-c)$ in both equations, we obtain

$$\frac{e^0}{e^R} = \frac{1 - \frac{1}{8e^R}(2R-c)}{1 - \frac{1}{8e^0}(-c)}.$$

By $e^0 \geq e^R$, the numerator of the right-hand side (RHS) has to be greater than the denominator of the RHS, or equivalently

$$\frac{2R-c}{e^R} < \frac{-c}{e^0},$$

which is a contradiction. □

7.2. Informational Naivety

Under IN, the expected payoffs from war of a player with resources R and 0 respectively equal

$$\left(\frac{1}{2}\frac{e_1^R}{e_1^R + e_2^R} + \frac{1}{2}\frac{e_1^R}{e_1^R + e_2^0}\right)\left(\frac{3}{2}R - c\right) - e_1^R \text{ and } \left(\frac{1}{2}\frac{e_1^0}{e_1^0 + e_2^R} + \frac{1}{2}\frac{e_1^0}{e_1^0 + e_2^0}\right)\left(\frac{1}{2}R - c\right) - e_1^0.$$

If $c = 0$, routine maximization steps yield the following unique type-symmetric equilibrium:

$$e^0 = \frac{7R}{64} \text{ and } e^R = \frac{21R}{64}. \tag{9}$$

---

[19] Throughout this subsection and the next one, the second-order conditions (SOCs) hold.

If $c \in [R/2, 3R/2]$, we immediately obtain $e_1^0 = e_2^0 = 0$, and plugging this result into the FOC of a player with resources R gives the following unique type-symmetric equilibrium:

$$e^0 = 0 \text{ and } e^R = \frac{3R - 2c}{16}. \tag{10}$$

For intermediate values of c, obtaining a closed-form solution for equilibrium efforts is less challenging than under IS and the type-symmetric equilibrium is unique. However, its derivation is routine and space consuming, and thus, we only write here the final result.

$$e^0 = \frac{8c^2 - 16cR + 7R^2}{64(R-c)^2}(R - 2c) \text{ and } e^R = \frac{8c^2 - 16cR + 7R^2}{64(R-c)^2}(3R - 2c). \tag{11}$$

Hence, the result corresponding to Lemma 1 (i.e., $e^R > e^0$) immediately follows from the comparison of the two above expressions.[20]

7.3. Comparative Statics

It is straightforward to verify the result of Proposition 1 (proved in a game-free setup) by plugging the equilibrium efforts back into individual payoffs. However, the advantage of a game-idiosyncratic model is the possibility of sharper predictions and comparative statics.

First, for every value of $c \geq 0$ and regardless of IS or IN, the equilibrium effort of a player strictly increases in their own resources (i.e., $e^R > e^0$), and consequently (*MonProb*) follows. This can be immediately verified in (7), (8), and Lemma 1 for IS and in (9), (10), and (11) for IN.

Second, we can compare for a given level of resources whether a player's effort is greater under IS or IN. If $c = 0$, a simple comparison of (7) and (9) shows that a player's effort is *smaller* under IS than under IN. If $c \in [R, 3R/2]$, a simple comparison of (8) and (10) shows that a player's effort is *greater* under IS than under IN. If c takes intermediate values (i.e., $c \in (0, R)$), the lack of tractability and multiplicity of equilibria in the case of IS does not allow an easy comparison.

The intuition why efforts could be greater under IS or under IN is as follows. On the one hand, a player affected by IN overestimates their expected payoff from war relative to IS predictions, and hence, they would a priori exert more effort under IN than under IS. On the other hand, a game-idiosyncratic approach makes a player affected by IN anticipate that their rival, being also affected by IN, expects a high payoff, and this discourages the first player's effort. The former effect turns out to be stronger when $c \in [R, 3R/2]$ (i.e., a player's effort is greater under IS than under IN), while the latter turns out to be stronger when $c = 0$ (i.e., a player's effort is greater under IN than under IS). This tention between opposing forces is clearly possible only when efforts are endogenous, which is the novelty of this section.

8. Discussion

Mutual optimism about the outcome of war is typically exogenously imposed in models on rationalist explanations for war. In this paper, we borrow from the economic literature a condition on the information processing capabilities of country leaders and show that such a condition gives rise to mutual optimism. Thus, in contrast to the canonical approach discussing mutual optimism as a source of outbreak of war, we take a step back and highlight a source of mutual optimism itself. We identify informational naivety as a source of mutual optimism: namely, country leaders fail to understand the correlation between other players' actions and their types despite understanding everything else in a conventional game theoretic sense, including the correct distribution of other players' actions and their types. We benchmark the setting with informational naivety to the one without (i.e., informational

---

[20] Steps identical to the proof of Lemma 1 would also show that $e^R > e^0$ in any interior type-symmetric equilibrium.

sophistication) and find that informational naivety unambiguously increases players' expected payoffs from war.

Interpreting players' expected payoffs from war as a proxy for the likelihood of war, as intuition and the literature suggest,[21] enhances the scientific payoff of the present exercise. Nonetheless, we remained agnostic about the specific channel through which larger expected payoffs from war increase the probability of war: for instance, larger expected payoffs from war could directly trigger an attack or could make it harder to reach an agreement that both players perceive as mutually advantageous.

It is important to compare our informational naivety to the canonical mutual optimism about the likelihood of victory, where subjective probabilities of victory sum to more than one.[22] To grasp the intuition, Fearon (1995) [5] considers a situation where two states bargain over the division of $100 and each has the outside option of going to war. If each expects that it surely would prevail at war, then each side's expected value for the war option is $80; as in Fearon's model, going to war entails a fixed cost of $20. Therefore, given these expectations, neither side will accept less than $80 in the bargaining, implying that no negotiated outcome is mutually preferred to war. More generally, suppose that state A expects to win with probability p, state B expects to win with probability r, and p and r sum to greater than one. Such conflicting expectations will certainly shrink and could eliminate any ex ante bargaining.

Both Section 2's and Fearon's examples depict noncomplex environments where irrational players compare in their minds war–peace payoffs. The two irrationalities are different in nature, and hence, the justifications proposed for the canonical mutual optimism do not automatically justify informational naivety. The canonical mutual optimism is traditionally, and still nowadays, justified with overconfidence: moods which cannot be grounded in fact result in a process by which nations evade reality (Blainey, 1988) [3]. Overconfidence has been proved to have strong predictive power in a number of fields other than conflict analysis. Informational naivety is also grounded on a single psychological principle, which, instead of being overconfidence, is the underappreciation of the informational content of other people's behavior (Eyster and Rabin, 2005) [11].

The canonical argument in support of informational naivety in fields other than conflicts is as follows. When augmenting a theoretical model by IN, its analytical result is typically checked to be consistent with the empirical observation. For instance, in auctions, the analytical result is that bidders overbid, which is in line with empirical findings. This empirical exercise typically sufficed as supportive evidence for at least two reasons: (i) the first-best direct observation of beliefs and, hence, miscalculations in line with IN is hardly available, and hence, empirically verifying the theoretical prediction is second-best, and (ii) IN is based on a well-established psychological principle. Clearly, points (i) and (ii) carry over to any setting with IN other than auctions and, hence, also to conflicts. Thus, similarly to auctions, we notice that the theoretical predictions of the model with IN (excessive bidding due to overestimation of the value of the object auctioned off conditional on victory or excessive war declarations due to the overestimation of the payoff from war) are consistent with real-world observation, missing the first-best direct evidence of IN beliefs. Finally, IN has similarly been proven to have significant predictive power in a number of fields other than conflict analysis: in fact, the predictions of informational naivety has been shown to be consistent with several real-life anomalous

---

[21] For pioneering works, see, for instance, Bueno de Mesquita and Lalman (1986) [26], Morrow (1989) [4], and Banks (1990) [27].
[22] A similar argument could be made for a systematic overestimation of the spoils of war: subjective estimations of the spoils of war sum to more than the objective stakes.

phenomena that conventional informational sophistication fails to capture, such as winner's curse in auctions,[23] various herd behaviours,[24] and trade in markets with adverse selection.[25]

Similarly to IN, the behavioural assumption of overestimation of likelihood of victory also suffers from missing any direct empirical evidence despite its theoretical prediction of excessive war declaration being widely observed. The reason is once again that directly observing and measuring such beliefs of country leaders is challenging. In fact, we are not aware of any empirical evidence that country leaders systematically overestimate the likelihood of victory. Nevertheless, as for our irrationality, scholars provided direct evidence that country leaders may not process information in an informationally sophisticated way: classical evidence of errors in processing information comes from the psychological international relations literature—in particular, see Jervis (1976) [28] and Jervis, Lebow, and Stein (1985) [29].[26] As pointed out by Fey and Ramsey (2007) [25], country leaders who have many responsibilities may face a volume of information that induces flaws in their learning."

We conclude with two remarks. First, informational naivety has been typically applied to rather complex strategic and informational environments, while we apply it to a simple correlation between two exogenous variables. However, recall that superimposing a game to our model, for example, endogenizing efforts as we did in Section 7, would not change the main result of overestimation of war payoffs as long as (*MonProb*) and (*MonSpoils*) hold. For this reason, existing evidence of informational naivety from complex environments encompasses our noncomplex environment too. Second, despite the high stakes of international conflicts instinctively suggesting that country leaders meticulously assess costs and benefits of a conflict, informational naivety has been successfully put forth as an explanation for failures in other high-stakes environments. For instance, when firms decide whether to enter a market, a firm neglecting that only firms sufficiently skilled decide to enter would overestimate their own profits from entry and, hence, over-enter: such a reference-group neglect generated by informational naivety could hence explain why most new businesses fail shortly after entry (Camerer and Lovallo, 1999) [30] . Inflated credit ratings are another high-stakes environment where, as pointed out by Skreta and Veldkamp (2009) [31], informational naivety could explain the upward bias in the rating of structured credit products, which is widely cited as one contributor to the crisis."

Funding: This research received no external funding.

Acknowledgments: I thank the Editor, Galina Zudenkova, and two anonymous referees for helpful comments and suggestions. I also thank Bharat Goel, Raphaela Hennigs, Kai Konrad, Jonas Send, and the participants at the XXXII Tax Day for useful discussion. All errors are my own.

Conflicts of Interest: The authors declare no conflict of interest.

References

1. Slantchev, B.L.; Tarar, A. Mutual Optimism as a Rationalist Explanation of War. *Am. J. Polit. Sci.* **2011**, *55*, 135–148. [CrossRef]
2. Wittman, D. How a War Ends: A Rational Model Approach. *J. Confl. Resolut.* **1979**, *23*, 743–763. [CrossRef]

---

[23] When bidders share a common but unknown value for the object at auction and receive private signals about such value, they tend to bid more than equilibrium theory predicts; this phenomenon is known as the winner's curse. A bidder wins if others bid sufficiently lower than them, which happens if others received private signals that are more negative than their own. A bidder who fails to draw such an inference between others' bids (actions) and signals (types) overestimates the value of the object and, hence, overbids (e.g., Kagel and Levin, 1986 [3]; Eyster and Rabin, 2005 [11]; and the references therein).

[24] Subjects disproportionately enter competitions on easy tasks (Moore and Cain, 2007) [32]. eBay sellers disproportionately choose to end their auctions during the times of day when more bidders are online (Simonsohn, 2010) [33]. Informationally naïve people herd with positive probability on incorrect actions (Eyster and Rabin, 2010) [14].

[25] If a prospective buyer fails to realize that a bid will only be accepted if the seller's valuation is less than the bid, then the buyer might incur a loss (e.g., Holt and Sherman, 1994) [10].

[26] See Lindsey (2018) [34] for a recent contribution overcoming the issue of the difficulty of observing country leaders' beliefs. See also Lai (2004) [35] and Bas and Schub (2016) [36] for similar empirical evidence. For laboratory experiments directly manipulating information, see Tingley and Wang (2010) [37] and Quek (2015) [38].

3. Blainey, G. *The Causes of War*; The Free Press: New York, NY, USA, 1988.
4. Morrow, J. Capabilities, Uncertainty, and Resolve: A Limited Information Model of Crisis Bargaining. *Am. J. Polit. Sci.* **1989**, *33*, 941–972. [CrossRef]
5. Fearon, J.D. Rationalist Explanations for War. *Int. Organ.* **1995**, *49*, 379–414. [CrossRef]
6. Werner, S. Negotiating the Terms of Settlement: War Aims and Bargaining Leverage. *J. Confl. Resolut.* **1998**, *42*, 321–343. [CrossRef]
7. Wagner, R.H. Bargaining and War. *Am. J. Polit. Sci.* **2000**, *44*, 469–484. [CrossRef]
8. Jackson, M.O.; Morelli, M. *The Reasons for Wars—An Updated Surveyin The Handbook on the Political Economy of War*; Coyne, C., Ed.; Edward Elgar: Northampton, MA, USA, 2011.
9. Kagel, J.H.; Levin, D. The Winner's Curse and Public Information in Common Value Auctions. *Am. Econ. Rev.* **1986**, *76*, 894–920.
10. Holt, C.A.; Shermanand, R. The Loser's Curse. *Am. Econ. Rev.* **1994**, *84*, 642–652.
11. Eyster, E.; Rabin, M. Cursed Equilibrium. *Econometrica* **2005**, *73*, 1623–1672. [CrossRef]
12. Jehiel, P. Analogy-Based Expectation Equilibrium. *J. Econ. Theory* **2005**, *123*, 81–104. [CrossRef]
13. Fudenberg, D.; Levine, D.K. Self-Confirming Equilibrium. *Econometrica* **1993**, *61*, 523–545. [CrossRef]
14. Eyster, E.; Rabin, M. Naive Herding in Rich-Information Settings. *Am. Econ. J. Microecon.* **2010**, *2*, 221–243. [CrossRef]
15. Jehiel, P.; Koessler, F. Revisiting Games of Incomplete Information with Analogy-Based Expectations. *Games Econ. Behav.* **2007**, *62*, 533–557. [CrossRef]
16. Ettinger, D.; Jehiel, P.A. Theory of Deception. *Am. Econ. J. Microecon.* **2010**, *2*, 1–20. [CrossRef]
17. Fudenberg, D. Advancing Beyond Advances in Behavioral Economics. *J. Econ. Lit.* **2006**, *44*, 694–711. [CrossRef]
18. Jackson, M.O.; Morelli, M. Political Bias and War. *Am. Econ. Rev.* **2007**, *97*, 1353–1373. [CrossRef]
19. Bueno de Mesquita, B. *The War Trap*; Yale University Press: New Haven, CT, USA, 1981.
20. Hörner, J.; Morelli, M.; Squintani, F. Mediation and Peace. *Rev. Econ. Stud.* **2015**, *82*, 1483–1501. [CrossRef]
21. Meirowitz, A.; Sartori, A.E. Strategic Uncertainty as a Cause of War. *Q. J. Polit. Sci.* **2008**, *3*, 327–352. [CrossRef]
22. Powell, R. Guns, Butter, and Anarchy. *Am. Polit. Sci. Rev.* **1993**, *87*, 115–132. [CrossRef]
23. Bueno de Mesquita, B.; Bruce, B.; Lalman, D. *War and Reason: Domestic and International Imperative*; Yale University Press: New Haven, CT, USA, 1992.
24. Fearon, J.D. Signaling versus the Balance of Power and Interests: An Empirical Test of a Crisis Bargaining Model. *J. Confl. Resolut.* **1994**, *38*, 236. [CrossRef]
25. Fey, M.; Ramsay, K.W. Mutual Optimism and War. *Am. J. Polit. Sci.* **2007**, *51*, 738–754. [CrossRef]
26. Bueno de Mesquita, B.; Bruce, B.; Lalman, D. Reason and War. *Am. Polit. Sci. Rev.* **1986**, *80*, 1113–1130. [CrossRef]
27. Banks, J.S. Equilibrium Behavior in Crisis Bargaining Games. *Am. J. Polit. Sci.* **1990**, *34*, 599–614. [CrossRef]
28. Jervis, R. *Perception and Misperception in International Relations*; Princeton University Press: Princeton, NJ, USA, 1976.
29. Jervis, R.; Lebow, R.N.; Stein, J.G. *Psychology and Deterrence*; The John Hopkins University Press: Baltimore, MD, USA, 1985.
30. Camerer, C.; Lovallo, D. Overconfidence and Excess Entry: An Experimental Approach. *Am. Econ. Rev.* **1999**, *89*, 306–318. [CrossRef]
31. Skreta, V.; Veldkamp, L. Ratings Shopping and Asset Complexity: A Theory of Ratings Inflation. *J. Monet. Econ.* **2009**, *56*, 678–695. [CrossRef]
32. Moore, D.A.; Cain, D.M. Overconfidence and Underconfidence: When and Why People Underestimate (and Overestimate) the Competition. *Organ. Behav. Hum. Decis. Process.* **2007**, *103*, 197–213. [CrossRef]
33. Simonsohn, U. eBay's Crowded Evenings: Competition Neglect in Market Entry Decisions. *Manag. Sci.* **2010**, *56*, 1060–1073. [CrossRef]
34. Lindsey, D. Mutual Optimism and Costly Conflict: The Case of Naval Battles in the Age of Sail. *J. Polit.* **2018**, *81*, forthcoming. [CrossRef]
35. Lai, B. The Effects of Different Types of Military Mobilization on the Outcome of International Crises. *J. Confl. Resolut.* **2004**, *48*, 211–229. [CrossRef]

36. Bas, M.; Schub, R. Mutual Optimism as a Cause of Conflict: Secret Alliances and Conflict Onset. *Int. Stud. Q.* **2016**, *60*, 552–564. [CrossRef]
37. Tingley, D.H. ; Wang, S.W. Belief Updating in Sequential Games of Two-Sided Incomplete Information: An Experimental Study of a Crisis Bargaining Model. *Q. J. Polit. Sci.* **2010**, *5*, 243–255. [CrossRef]
38. Quek, K. Rationalist Experiments on War. *Polit. Sci. Res. Methods* **2015**, *5*, 123–142. [CrossRef]

 © 2019 by the authors. Licensee MDPI, Basel, Switzerland. This article is an open access article distributed under the terms and conditions of the Creative Commons Attribution (CC BY) license (http://creativecommons.org/licenses/by/4.0/).

MDPI
St. Alban-Anlage 66
4052 Basel
Switzerland
Tel. +41 61 683 77 34
Fax +41 61 302 89 18
www.mdpi.com

Games Editorial Office
E-mail: games@mdpi.com
www.mdpi.com/journal/games

www.ingramcontent.com/pod-product-compliance
Lightning Source LLC
LaVergne TN
LVHW072001080526
838202LV00064B/6813